WINNING

a story of grief and renewal

HARRIET HODGSON

North Carolina

The information in this book is not intended to serve as a replacement for professional medical advice or counseling. Any use of the information in this book is at the reader's sole discretion. The author and publisher disclaim any and all liability rising directly or indirectly from the use or application of information in this book. A medical/health care professional should be consulted regarding your specific situation. While every effort has been made to ensure the information in this book is the most current, new research findings may invalidate some data.

Published in the United States by WriteLife Publishing
(an imprint of Boutique of Quality Books Publishing, Inc.)

Library of Congress Number: 2023939762

978-1-60808-291-9 (p)
978-1-60808-292-6 (e)

Book design by Robin Krauss, www.bookformatters.com
Cover design by Rebecca Lown, www.rebeccalowndesign.com

First Editor: Andrea Vande Vorde
Second Editor: Allison Itterly

Praise for *Winning*
and Author Harriet Hodgson

"*Winning: A Story of Grief and Renewal* by Harriet Hodgson is a beautifully written memoir of her life with her deceased husband and daughter. Harriet packs a lot of great information, tools, and resources in less than 200 pages. I highly recommend *Winning* for anyone who has experienced loss."

– David Roberts, LMSW, bereaved parent and co-author of *When the Psychology Professor Met the Minister.*

"*Winning* by Harriet Hodgson is engaging and descriptive— she brings you into her life as she lived it. Harriet has done an excellent job of telling how important it is not to bandage grief but live through it. She has done a superb job on this book. We are walking with her on the journey. Well done."

– Mary and Darwyn Tri, co-leaders of *The Compassionate Friends,* Rochester, MN chapter.

"*Winning* is a remarkable book, beautifully written about grief and renewal from grief. The book captivates the reader and draws them into thinking about their own grief issues. The author describes the different types of grief in detail. Her own grief includes losing a daughter in a car accident, adopting and raising her daughter's twin grandchildren, and seven years of caring for her physician husband after a dissecting aneurysm left him without the use of his legs. Hodgson has been described as a

National Treasure for the remarkable person that she is. *Winning* is a gem."

> – David E. Dines, MD, Emeritus Professor of Medicine,
> Mayo Clinic, Rochester, MN.

"Harriet Hodgson's *Winning: A Story of Grief and Renewal* is her best masterpiece. I am in awe of a woman, eighty-plus years young, who has suffered so many tragedies, has given so much back to her family and to the grieving community. *Winning* is a legacy to Harriet's family, with lovely memories of her beloved husband John, her parents, her beloved daughter, and other family members. The book is a raw, honest, and inspiring grief journey filled with hope and resilience. For anyone who has experienced any loss, [it is]chock full of resources, tips, and Harriet's unwavering wisdom. As Harriet states, "Many of life's questions have no answers." For over forty years of sharing grief knowledge, "I need to accept the things I couldn't change." *Winning* is a beautiful complication of Harriet at her best."

> – Judy Lipson, author *Celebration of Sisters: It is Never Too
> Late to Grieve*. Keynote speaker, The Bereaved Parents
> of the USA National Conference 2023.

"Harriet Hodgson has the gift of good grieving. In this heartfelt and helpful book, she shares her unique story of multiple family losses. She also shows how one can thrive while bereaved. Harriet is a keen, creative, compassionate guide."

> – Neil Chethik, author of *Father Loss: How Sons of
> All Ages Come to Terms with the Deaths of Their Dads*.

"Once you start *Winning* you can't put it down. It is honest and riveting. The way Hodgson ties scientific information with her experience is amazing. I think every school of nursing and every school of psychiatric nursing should have this book."

– Ruth Kahn, PhD, Emeritus Director of Nursing Education,
National Institutes of Health.

"*Winning* by Harriet Hodgson is a true story about specific ways to deal with grief. Each type of grief can leave deep emotional scars. They can be healed by actively facing grief and pain. Harriet discusses ways to bring about a real-life renewal."

– George Allen, MD, Emeritus Mayo Clinic staff physician,
Rochester, MN.

"Having lost our daughter to health complications at the age of 50 in 2020, I wasn't sure I needed to read another book on death and dying. But I found Harriet Hodgson's new book, *Winning*, to be very helpful since parents never really stop grieving the loss of a child. Hodgson writes a very personal and informal book about dealing with the deaths of several close family members in a short span of time. . . . The reader can always find something that strikes a chord that will invite thought and conversation. She is open about her struggle to find new meaning and activities (like doodling) in her own life after years of being a caregiver. Hodgson's experience during COVID was interesting to me since our daughter's death occurred in the early days of COVID when we were isolated in our apartment for several weeks. . . . In *Winning*, readers will feel they have found a comforting friend they can relate to rather than a lecturer."

– Alan Dollerschell, Retired Coordinator,
Rochester Community and Technical College Library.

"This is a book you need to read. In clear, no-nonsense prose we explore Harriet Hodgson's staggering encounters with the challenges of grief. We experience her clear-eyed decisions and active responses. If you're experiencing overwhelming sorrow after the loss of someone near and dear, this book just might help you."

– B. Beery, PhD, Curriculum Director, retired, Rochester, MN Public Schools.

"Extremely well-written, this is not some abstract theoretical treatise but the stuff of actual lived experience. It is this which gives *Winning* added authority and validity. You are honest about yourself, and your wisdom is tinged with a personal truth. I wish you great success with this honest, life-affirming book."

– Michael York, Actor, Author, and Narrator

This one is for my beloved John:
a devoted husband, father, grandfather,
great-grandfather, and physician.

Death will be the loser.
Life will be the winner.
I will make it so.

Table of Contents

Foreword

Winning by Harriet Hodgson took me by surprise. After working with grieving people for over 13 years there is a certain sameness in what even the most skilled writers have to say. *Winning* is an exception.

Harriet has been processing severe grief for a long time and she is generous in sharing her personal story.

She has survived the death of both her daughter and then later her daughter's husband, which led her to lovingly raise her fraternal twin grandchildren. Then, after many years of a loving and devoted marriage, she became first a caregiver to her beloved husband, and then his widow. These are only some of the deaths Harriet has experienced.

The author of more than 44 books, her style is both beautiful, easy to understand, and relate to. Harriet interweaves her personal story with practical actions to take and ways to change patterns of thought. There are no platitudes here. Instead, her words are genuinely helpful.

The topics she discusses in *Winning* are wide-ranging, everything from anticipatory grief, to loneliness, to grief brain, to grief heart, to permission to laugh, to forming a new relationship with deceased loved ones, and so much more. Her stories (some of them funny) and grief research will touch your mind and heart.

At the beginning, Harriet writes, "Death will be the loser. Life will be the winner. I will make it so." Then she delivers the many pathways that even someone as doubtful as I am, can understand and follow. Choosing life and joy while grieving can seem impossible.

Winning makes this not only possible, but probable.

> – Jan Warner, Author of *Grief Day by Day:*
> *Simple Practices* and *Daily Guidance for Living*
> *with Loss*, www.Facebook.com/GriefSpeaksOut,
> www.griefdaybyday.com.

Preface

I've been a freelancer for forty-four years. In 2022 I had two books published: *Daisy a Day: Hope for a Grieving Heart*, a concise, helpful, and hopeful resource for the bereaved, and *First Steps, First Snow*, a children's picture book based on a true experience.

"Well, that's it," I muttered to myself. "Forty-four books are enough. I'm eighty-seven years old. Maybe it's time to retire."

But the idea of retiring was so upsetting that I gave myself a pep talk. The talk didn't quell my doubts. What would I do if I retired? What would I do week after week? Month after month? Year after year?

I have the type of mind that needs to be busy. Really busy. Heck, I even write in my sleep. I frame sentences, review structure, consider word choices, and see words on paper, all while snoring. Then I awaken suddenly, turn on the computer, type the sentences, and save the document. To my chagrin, I'm often writing at four in the morning, and this affects the rest of the day. Everything seems a little "off."

There's not much going on at the crack of dawn. The moon is still out, sometimes full, sometimes half, sometimes a "fingernail," as my mother-in-law called it. Stars are fading, and as night becomes day, the sky turns from inky black to the color of gray flannel. Train tracks are close to my building, and I can hear the whistle: rhythmic blasts to warn drivers and pedestrians. The whistle is a lonely, yet comforting, sound that tells me others are awake.

I live in Rochester, Minnesota, home base of Mayo Clinic. A block away is Methodist Hospital, which is part of Mayo. From my living room window, I can see the helicopter landing pad, the orange windsock, and green signal lights. Most of the time, Mayo One lands there, but I also see helicopters from other medical centers. I use binoculars to see the logos on the planes.

A helicopter that comes from the east between my building and a Mayo Clinic building makes me nervous. It gets so close that I feel like I could hand the pilot a cup of coffee. Though the flight path is safe, the helicopter flies too close for comfort and I start to worry. But I have seen many safe helicopter landings in good weather and bad.

A small park across the street is filled with historic oak trees. The trees were there when Rochester was founded in 1854. Season after season, day after day, thousands of crows come to the park to sleep. So many crows land on the trees that no leaves are visible. The trees become black silhouettes. In the early morning, I hear crows cawing at each other and watch them swarm into the sky and head for farms outside the city.

As interesting as these events are, they don't keep me from writing. Writing is my passion; writing is my life.

I thought I'd made peace with retirement until I received an email from the editor of a grief website. The editor said he didn't know anyone else who had experienced so much tragedy and raised twin grandchildren while grieving. He thought I should write a memoir.

What an idea. What a challenge.

Writing is hard work, and despite years of experience and a track record as an author, the idea of writing a memoir was daunting. Besides, I knew many people who started memoirs and never finished them. My mother-in-law was one of those people.

She struggled with the first chapter for months and became so tangled in a web of names and dates and events that she quit writing. I didn't need to repeat her experience.

Yet the idea of a memoir was appealing. Years ago, I wrote a history of Rochester, and it sold well. In fact, it went back to press three times. Chapter topics included agriculture, education, healthcare, and technology. Instead of a chronological approach, I used a topical approach. For example, the technology chapter was titled, "Computers Amidst the Corn Rows." The topical approach worked before, so maybe it could work again.

The editor's email made my mind race. I could tell my grief story, the challenges I faced, and the healing steps I took. It would be an honest, heartfelt story. Each chapter would focus on a grief issue and healing steps that would help others. I brainstormed a list of possible book titles and read them aloud. Which sounded good? Which sounded awful? Soon my mind was going in circles.

As I had done many times before, I let my subconscious deal with the problem. My subconscious had never failed me. If I was patient, a title would eventually surface. One day, while I was making the bed, the title flashed in my mind: *Winning*. The one-word title was strong, upbeat, and easy to remember.

The title idea transported me back in time, and I thought about my daughter's death. A week after she died, I sat down at the computer and poured out my grief in words. I remembered tears streaming down my face. I remembered the decision I'd made that day—a decision that altered my outlook, my healing path, and my life. These simple words became my mantra.

Death will be the loser. Life will be the winner. I will make it so.

Yes, I've suffered multiple losses and learned from each one. Grief forced me to grow as a person, have more compassion, and develop resilience. My deceased loved ones would want me to be happy. *Winning* sounded like a happy, strong title. On a whim, I sent it to the editor, and he replied quickly.

"I love it!"

I cheered when I read this. If the title was good enough for him, it was good enough for me. The more I thought about *Winning,* the more I liked it. Once I had the title, the words came so quickly I could barely keep up with them. Evidently, I'd been storing ideas for years.

This book has a dual purpose:

The first purpose is to help you create a healing path.

The second purpose is to help you believe in the future.

Hope is the theme of this book, and it's part of every chapter. While I was writing *Winning*, I pictured a white candle of hope with a flickering yellow flame. As I struggled with grief, however, my imaginary flame sputtered and almost went out. Yet the spark was still evident and waiting to flare. That spark kept me going.

Winning is a story about coping with multiple losses, living with them, believing in a future, and creating a new life. Each chapter includes tips for coping with grief. If you're at the start of your journey, or you have been grieving for a long time, my story may be helpful. At the end, I hope you believe you're capable of winning and will think of yourself as a winner.

Instead of merely surviving grief, you have the power to thrive and create a rewarding future—the future you deserve.

Chapter 1

Looking Grief in the Face

Grief is a strange place—one I didn't want to visit. I'd experienced grief before, and each loss wounded me. I'm sorry to say this, but I was all too familiar with emergency phone calls, newspaper obituaries, grief rituals, memorial services, and all the paperwork that went with them. I wasn't proud of this knowledge.

In his book *Life After Loss*, Bob Deits says nobody wants to be good at grief.[1] That "nobody" includes me. Yet time and again, I looked grief in the face, and it wasn't a pleasant experience. Grief was nasty, but I learned to live with it. As the years passed, grief seeped into my soul.

When I shared my story with others, however, the reaction was always disbelief. "Hollywood would never accept your story. It's too emotional," my friend said. She was right. Sometimes I hardly believed my own story. But grieving people need to tell their stories and say their loved ones' names.

Telling my story helped me heal. Though I said my loved ones' names and told stories about them, I didn't see the big picture of my grief. Grieving for multiple losses was like assembling a puzzle. I had some of the pieces, not all, and wasn't sure how they fit together. Did I have all the pieces I needed?

Grief experts think it's helpful to make a grief timeline. I'm a visual learner, so I followed this advice. I drew a line through

---

1 Bob Deits, *Life After Loss: A Practical Guide to Renewing Your Life After Experiencing Major Loss* (Boston, MA: Da Capo Lifelong Press, 2009), 109.

the center of a piece of paper, and I wrote the names of deceased loved ones and friends above the line. Below the line, I wrote the dates of their deaths. The timeline included the death of Timmy, our black cocker spaniel, who died when I was in fifth grade.

If I didn't know the date of death, I made an educated guess. My timeline showed a grief cluster in 2007. Four family members died in a row: my daughter, my father-in-law, my brother, and my daughter's husband. No wonder I think of 2007 as the year of death.

Experiencing Multiple Losses

My daughter and father-in-law died on the same weekend in February. When I saw their photos in the obituary page of the newspaper, and the family name printed twice, I sobbed and sobbed. I wondered if I would ever stop crying. It was like a punch to the gut. I took the punch with my eyes wide open and kept them open. For if I looked aside, even for a few minutes, things could get worse. My troubled life could become more troubled. I didn't need that and kept telling myself, "I will get through this."

The death of a child is like no other. When my oldest daughter, Helen, died in a tragic car accident, leaving behind her husband and twin children, my husband John and I were overcome with grief. We cried for hours, stopped for an hour or so, and cried again. I cried so much that I was almost cried out. The sun was setting, and there was an orange glow in the western sky. I looked at the white birch trees in the side yard and watched the sky darken.

"It's time for dinner," I announced. "What would you like?"

"I don't want anything," John replied.

"Well, you need to eat something," I reasoned. "How about scrambled eggs?"

"Okay," he agreed. "But I don't want a lot."

I scrambled an egg for each of us and fixed some fresh fruit. We ate at the kitchen table in front of a bay window that overlooked the yard. Sitting at the table with John was always interesting. Herds of deer ran by. (Yes, herds roamed our neighborhood.) A variety of birds came to feed on our berry bushes. Stray mallards walked across the back lawn. We even saw a flock of pheasants.

Eating at the kitchen table was like having front-row seats at nature's show. We didn't look for wildlife that day. Grief was the only thing we saw, and we ate in silence. This was upsetting because we always had news to share. When I cleared the plates, the eggs were gone but the fruit remained. All we could eat was an egg.

I served coffee after "dinner," such as it was. John drank all of his coffee. I only had a few sips of mine. If I drank anymore, I thought I'd barf.

The family deaths kept coming, and my father-in-law was next. My daughter died on Friday and Dad died on Sunday of the same weekend. Dad was the patriarch of the family, and his death affected all family members. There were so many things I would miss about Dad: his intelligence, his wisdom, his humor, and his stories. Dad told stories about his childhood, his years in Lima, Peru, his medical practice, and his family. What concerned me the most after his death was the fact that the main source of our family history was gone.

Just as I was beginning to feel better, another loved one would die. Like the lyrics of a country song, I took a few steps forward and a few steps back. Life pulled me in opposite directions so hard that I thought I'd snap. This was exhausting. Life was exhausting. I didn't know myself anymore.

My emotions jumped around like crickets on a summer night. A jump here, a jump there. Many emotions were opposites:

exhaustion and energy, pessimism and optimism, despair and hope, to name a few. Dealing with these feelings was painful.

My brother, and only sibling, was the third family member to die in 2007. He died about eight weeks after Helen died. My brother was five years older than me. We had been estranged for several years, and I never knew why. I continued to send him birthday cards but never heard from him. Then, out of the blue, my brother called me one day. He had cancer and wondered if John could help him get an appointment at Mayo Clinic in Jacksonville.

John helped my brother get an appointment, and he underwent a series of cancer treatments. We thought my brother would live. Sadly, after he completed treatment, my brother had a heart attack in the night and died.

Grief Sparks Childhood Memories

My brother's death brought back a lot of memories we shared in childhood. World War II was raging at the time, and my brother and I would play war games. I was always the enemy, while my brother was always the hero. He put model plane kits together and hung the models from his bedroom ceiling. He studied flashcards of enemy aircraft. Each card had a black silhouette of a plane on it, perfect for quick identification.

Radio was our main source of family entertainment. For months, my parents saved money to buy a radio. The radio was nothing like today's modern radios. It was about five feet tall, made of mahogany with wooden legs, a large dial, and a cloth-covered soundbox. The radio had a place of honor in our living room, and we gathered around it.

I loved listening to the radio, so much that I scratched my name on the front with a pencil, pressing as hard as I could.

Of course, this damaged the finish, but my parents never said a word. They'd bought one radio and couldn't afford to buy another. Even though I continued to listen to programs, I felt ashamed every time I sat by the radio. I didn't understand why I had felt compelled to scratch my name on the front of it.

My brother and I used to listen to *The Shadow* and *Captain Midnight*. The lead-in to *The Shadow* program was dramatic. The announcer described a mysterious scenario in a compelling voice (which I can still hear), asked if listeners knew about it, and ended with: "The Shadow knows." The announcer's voice scared me.

We were excited when our Captain Midnight decoder rings arrived in the mail. (I think the rings cost twenty-five cents each.) After we decoded the first message, "Tune in next week," we weren't as excited. What a disappointment. Even though I lost all interest in my decoder ring, I still listened to the programs.

My family didn't have a television, so going to the library was entertainment. The public library was within walking distance, and we checked out as many books as we could carry. I would carry a wobbly tower of books, a dozen or so, and was glad when I reached our house. My brother and I read for hours, and I think my love of reading came from him.

Our parents bought each of us a special gift, something we would remember all our lives. I received a spinet piano made by Sohmer, a well-known company at the time. An experimental model, the piano had a smaller soundboard and superb tone. I took piano lessons from a family friend.

Later, when I was a junior in high school, I took voice lessons. The student with the lesson ahead of me was being trained to project her voice over a live orchestra, something I never learned. Sometimes I arrived early for my lesson, heard the student singing, and was impressed with her voice. When I first started lessons, my teacher thought I was a dramatic soprano. Subsequent lessons revealed I was a lyric soprano, the most common type.

My parents gave my brother a twelve-and-a-half-foot Sandpiper sailboat. He taught himself how to sail and became such an excellent sailor that he taught classes. But I never learned how to sail because I was the crew. I carried the anchor, tied ropes to cleats, and ducked under the boom when he yelled, "Coming about!"

I missed my brother. I wished I could see him again and repair our broken relationship, but it was too late. My brother was gone.

John and I flew to Long Island, New York, to attend my brother's memorial service. We were still reeling from Helen's and my father-in-law's deaths. Now we had to process a third death in the family. How much tragedy could a family take?

"I'm afraid we're getting used to this," John confided.

"Me too," I whispered. "Me too."

The fourth family member to pass away was Helen's former husband, the twins' father. He died in a different car accident. One of the twins called and said in a quivering voice, "There's been another crash. Daddy is in the emergency room." Thankfully, the hospital was only a few blocks away and we were there in minutes—just in time to learn the twins' father had died. Suddenly, the twins were orphans, and we were their caregivers.

Becoming a Legal Guardian

The year 2007 was terrible. "Why is this happening to us?" my granddaughter had asked. I couldn't answer her question. Our family was at a crossroads, a time when life and death collided, and the collision was harsh. I tried to keep a calm expression on my face, but I was an emotional wreck on the inside.

If I felt this badly, I wondered how the twins felt. They were fifteen years old at the time, a difficult age for kids and parents. Since there was nothing more we could do, we left the hospital and went outside to make some plans. John and I stood together, and the twins stood several feet away. My grandson was protective of his sister. I couldn't hear their entire conversation but heard the beginning.

"Moving in with Grandma and Grandpa makes sense," my grandson began. "We know them and know the house." The twins moved in with us that night.

Our Cape Cod house turned out to be perfect for a blended family. The house had four bedrooms—three on the top floor and one on the lower level. The room that became my granddaughter's was the largest. The bed was a wrought-iron antique, a gift we received from a relative when we got married. We had loved the design of the bed, but not the worn mattress with a picture of a bedbug in the middle and the words, "Vermin-Proof." When I'd first seen the mattress, I was aghast.

"Yuck! I married you for better or for worse," I joked to John. "Not for vermin-proof!" He didn't like the mattress either, so we chucked it and bought a new mattress. Then when we gave the bed to our granddaughter, we bought another new mattress for her. Because the antique bed was an odd size, the mattress had to be custom-made. A local factory made it and gave us a discount with free delivery when the owner learned John was a Vietnam veteran. We appreciated the gesture.

My grandson's room was the smallest. He slept in the bed that had been his mother's, which had electronic controls. I bought him a blue bedspread because blue was his favorite color. I hung a wildlife print over his bed and a family photo on the opposite wall. I hoped the photo would be a source of comfort and a reminder of family support.

Years later, when I was writing a book about raising

grandkids, I asked my grandson what he thought of his bedroom. "I was glad to have a place to sleep," my practical grandson answered.

Getting legal guardianship of the twins took months. We hired a lawyer and went to court twice, once to ask for guardianship and another to receive it. Several people were ahead of us on the court docket. Witnessing the proceedings was an emotional experience. One woman asked for money to feed her children, and the judge granted her request. Another case was about obtaining legal representation for a man who had Alzheimer's disease. The judge called him on speakerphone. I heard the conversation and could tell the man needed help. When the conversation ended, the judge appointed a court lawyer. At that point, I was an emotional wreck and wondered if I'd be able to think, let alone speak.

Our lawyer summarized our request for guardianship and the judge took notes. I wished I could see what he was writing. John and I were granted legal guardianship of our grandchildren.

The teenage years can be tough for both parents and kids. Now when I look back, I think we learned more from the twins than they learned from us. Though we worried about parenting teens again, our worries were unfounded. The twins were good kids. Like all teenagers, they invited friends over for dinner and had sleepovers. Our quiet house became a busy, bustling, noisy place, and I loved it.

I saw life through my grandchildren's eyes. Life was fresh and new and exciting again.

Many say *change* is the constant of life. I think surprise is another constant. At that point in my life, I was sixty-seven years old and had coped with many surprises, some so sad I was immobile, some so happy I wanted to cheer from the rooftops. The year of multiple losses was the beginning of a winding grief journey with starts, stops, and detours. My goal was to keep moving forward.

Steps to Healing

Today, I can see what I accomplished. To quote popular advertising words, I was a "new and improved" version of myself. And yes, I was proud of this person. The struggle was hard, but I was still standing. Even better, I was living a new and exciting life. How did I get there?

I went with the pain.
I learned about grief.
I cried when I felt like it.
I tackled painful tasks.
I learned from my mistakes.
I adapted day by day.
I followed my healing path.
I created a new and happy life.

Grief has many symptoms, and I had them all: crying spells, mood swings, mental confusion, poor hygiene (like not styling my hair), poor eating habits, loss of appetite, weight gain or loss (I gained), poor or interrupted sleep, dry mouth (from all the crying), new aches and pains, poor decision-making, inability to concentrate, fragmented recall (I couldn't remember what I read), and exhaustion. I was barely functioning.

Coping With the Loss of My Husband

On November 28, 2020, I looked grief in the face once again when John died. I think of myself as a recent widow and always will. John and I met on a blind date shortly after we started college. I was seventeen and John, being an "older man," was eighteen years old. We were college sweethearts for four years and married for sixty-three years. "I think our marriage will last," John said with a smile on his face.

Our love for each other was tender and deep. It must have been obvious because people commented on our marriage.

"Robert and I don't have the kind of relationship you and John have," a friend admitted. "We love each other but aren't as close."

This admission surprised me. I couldn't think of anything to say, so I said nothing.

John and I knew each other well before we married. This knowledge was the foundation of our relationship. We knew each other's likes and dislikes, the values we lived by, our long-term goals, and favorite foods. Knowing these things made our marriage solid. John almost knew me better than I knew myself. We often talked about our long-term marriage.

"I've known you longer than any other person in the world," John said.

"And I've known you longer than any other person in the world," I repeated.

Without John, however, my days were different, lonely, and shallow. His death, and the deaths of family members, left huge gaps in my life. With determination, support, and research, I learned from these losses, created a personal healing path, and kept moving forward.

John's death had a profound effect on my life. Grief made me stronger and more determined to live a happy life in honor of him. Living life without John wouldn't be easy, but I was determined to do it. John wasn't with me physically, but he was with me emotionally, and this thought strengthened me. Because of grief, I've said things I never thought I'd say. Because of grief, I've done things I never thought I'd do.

Several months after John died, I accepted a job offer from a grief website. My tasks included asking authors to write for us and share excerpts from their books, and suggesting authors for radio, television, and podcasts. I didn't have time to read every author's book, but I was familiar with their names and work. These authors were colleagues, people who understood why I write, what I write, and what I read.

I thought John would have approved of my new job. In my mind, I heard him cheering for me. When I was alone, I cheered for myself. But my cheers dwindled when I heard the African American spiritual, "Hush, Somebody's Callin' My Name."

When Grief Comes Knockin'

The song is about the fear of death. A line from the first verse says, "Grief came knockin' at my door." This line sounded like it was written for me. I read it three times and a different word stood out each time.

The first time I heard, "*Grief* came knockin' at my door."
The second time I heard, "Grief came *knockin'* at my door."
The third time I heard, "Grief came knockin' at *my* door."

The word *my* stood out because it was personal. Grief didn't just knock at my door; it banged loudly, again and again, with a heavy fist. The last line of the verse ends with a question: "What shall I do? What shall I do?"

I didn't know what to do. In time, I would find out.

The Stress of Grief

I wanted life to stop and wait for me. It didn't. There were meals to fix, clothes to wash, errands to run, and bills to pay.

"Slow down, life!" I wanted to shout. "Give me time to catch up."

Life handed me a despicable plot, yet I had the power to write a decent ending, one that would lead me forward. I didn't know my path included a few detours.

In February 2007, shortly after our daughter died, I went to the grocery store. Somehow— and I'm not sure how—I bought all the items on my list. This small triumph proved that my mind was functioning. I loaded the groceries into the trunk of my car, got in, and started to back out.

Bump.

Oh my gosh, what had I hit? When I looked behind me, I saw a man get out of his car and walk toward me.

"You hit my bumper," he said in accented English. "Look, your car is newer than mine. See all the scratches on my car? There aren't any scratches on yours."

I sensed a lawsuit coming, and my hands began to sweat. Still in a daze, I touched the man's hand and said, "I'm so sorry. Two members of my family just died, and I'm stressed. Are you okay?"

The man stared at me for a few seconds. The angry expression on his face changed to one of understanding. "I'm fine," he mumbled and walked back to his car. His wife was sitting in the passenger seat. She waved and smiled as they drove away.

I never told John about this incident. He was stressed, I was stressed, and we didn't need any more stress in our lives. However, I did bring up the subject of driver safety. John and I were safe drivers. We fastened our seatbelts, obeyed speed limits, and always left margins of safety. Because we were afraid of having an accident, we came up with a plan. Before we left the house, we would determine our roles. One of us would be the driver and the other the lookout. Every time we used the car, we swapped roles.

We could have asked relatives or neighbors to drive us, but we didn't. Our schedules were erratic, our emotions were raw, and we didn't want to impose on others. The real reason, and perhaps the most important one, was that we didn't know how we would feel from one minute to the next. The driver lookout plan worked well, and we used it for months.

Taking Proactive Steps toward Healing

Team sports have offense and defense. Being proactive was a way for us to play offense. A daily routine provided structure, so we stuck with our routine. We went to bed at the same time, got up at the same time, and ate at the same time. We cried when we needed to, no matter where we were or what we were doing. This was another proactive step.

I would act normal for a few hours, and then, without any warning, I would burst into tears. My face became red and splotchy. Several times, I pulled the car over so I could cry. After I cried, I felt like a weight had been lifted from my shoulders. Instead of being ashamed, I was proud of my tears because they were signs of love.

Thanking friends for their kindness was another proactive step. The postman delivered dozens of sympathy cards, many with handwritten notes. I read the cards and comments until reading became too painful. I stashed the cards in a box and put the box away. I planned to read them when I felt stronger. I finally did six months later. Friends and neighbors sent us flowers. One bouquet stands out in my memory. The all-white arrangement contained a variety of flowers. Even in my shocked state, I realized the arrangement was stunning. I sent a short thank-you note to the couple who had sent the white bouquet. Today, thinking about the artistic, calming bouquet brings tears to my eyes.

Loss of Control

After our daughter died, every aspect of our lives—eating, feeling, thinking, sleeping, working, socializing, and simply being—was out of control. Instead of living *my* life, I felt like I'd been dropped into someone else's life by mistake. John and I were adrift in a sea of grief, with no life preservers in sight. My heart ached for him. My heart ached for me.

I looked terrible, and John seemed lost in thought. He stared vacantly into space. John's brown eyes saw nothing, and at the same time, saw everything. The death of a child was like no other, and I'd never seen John like this. He looked shocked, worn out, and hopeless.

"This is too much," I said gently. "Our lives are out of control."

"What can we control?" John asked.

Though our interests differed, John and I had the same values and humor. We thought alike and even said the same sentences. Our memory systems were different, and comparing memories was always a surprise. John remembered a specific highway, its number, and how it curved around the mountain. I remembered the white clapboard church by the side of the road and a field of sunflowers.

John was the scientist; I was the artist.

Each of us was half of the other, and together we were whole. We had worked together for years and worked our way through grief together. To give myself breaks from grief, I read magazines, watched television, or baked. I'm a made-from-scratch cook, and baking was relaxing. I wasn't proud of the results, darn it, I was ashamed of them.

Grief distracted me. I measured ingredients incorrectly, left out ingredients, burned food, and had total failures. This wasn't like me, and I apologized to John for my lack of skills.

"You must think I can't boil water," I declared.

John's reply was something he said many times: "I've never had a bad meal in this house."

Regaining Control

Life gave us three options. Option one was to wait to be rescued. Option two was to rescue ourselves. Option three was to sit around and wait to die. We chose option two. Grief is part of being human, and we all experience it. While I understood this intellectually, I didn't understand it emotionally because death found me.

Despite the unpredictable pattern of bad days and good days, life started to look better. In the darkness of grief, I saw a glimmer of hope and walked toward it. I wouldn't merely survive, I promised myself, but I would thrive. John and I tackled painful tasks together. We bought a burial plot for our daughter, chose a headstone, sent her obituary to the newspaper, planned her memorial service, and hosted a luncheon afterward. I don't know how we managed to do these things, but we did.

Life started to improve and, to use a flight term, leveled off a bit. John and I thought we were doing well. After all that had happened, we were still standing. Our education, talents, and jobs were intact. Our minds functioned well—not all the time, but most of the time. Most importantly, we were together.

John had officially retired from Mayo Clinic and continued to work on a contract basis. Raising grandchildren forced him to quit work altogether. He had to manage his deceased mother's estate, our granddaughter's estate, our grandson's estate, and our estate. Estate management was his new job. The paperwork was extensive, but he still kept the numbers straight.

A Team Effort

We divided our duties along traditional lines. John handled legal responsibilities and the twins' finances, and he drove the kids to school in the morning. I took charge of home stuff, school events, and picking up the twins after school. To avoid a highway filled with cars and buses, I waited for the twins at a gas station on the other side of the highway. A walking bridge over the highway enabled kids to cross safely. I watched kids walk across the bridge after school was out. Most of the kids were chatting and happy. The twins were quiet and sad.

Many factors influenced the length of my grief: my relationship with the deceased, the length of our relationship, their personality and interests, the cause of death, past experience with grief, and the time interval between the deaths. Coping with multiple losses was harder than coping with one. For one thing, the process took longer, and there were so many things to consider, like disbursing possessions and what to do with Helen's house, and I became confused. I couldn't cope with multiple losses alone.

From the first day we met, John and I were a team. If we worked harder, we could regain some control over our lives. Not much, but some. Every ounce of control counted. Our twin grandchildren were our top priority. Our job was to protect them, guide them, and love them more each day. As the years passed, we merged into a "grandfamily," a term that comes from the Association of Retired Persons (AARP). The term fit us perfectly.

The twins became our kids. With gentle care, we helped them through high school, and they graduated with honors. We helped them through college, and they graduated with honors. My granddaughter married a minister. They have two sons and live in Michigan. Though miles separate us, we stay in touch via email and are still a grandfamily.

My grandson is a radiology resident at Mayo Clinic in Rochester, Minnesota. If I need help, he is at the door. He checks on me and takes me out to dinner. If something needs to be fixed, my grandson does it. Many grandparents who raise grandchildren don't have happy endings like mine. I'm so proud of my grandkids that I'd do cartwheels if I still could.

Understanding Grief

My grief experience helped me understand the grief process. I was aware of how voices carried in different places. One time, after a memorial service for a church member had just ended, I heard someone remark, "She's young. She'll find someone else." The widow overheard this and grimaced. I felt sick for her.

Hearing the remark made me more careful about what I said, where I said it, and how I said it.

Non-grievers don't always understand grief. They tracked time differently than I did. Many people thought I should be over grief in a few weeks. Really? I didn't understand why anyone would say this, especially after four family members died. Even kind, thoughtful, and helpful people misunderstood the path and length of grief.

In 2007 a friend asked, "Your daughter died about a year ago, right?"

"She died three months ago," I replied.

"Oh," the woman said and walked away.

My friends lived life in one time zone, and I lived life in another. Our zones were far apart and would never meet. I don't say this critically. People who aren't grieving have busy lives, but life comes to a standstill for those who are grieving. I envied those whose lives were normal and progressing.

Finding Strength in Times of Weakness

"You're a strong person," was a sentence I often heard. Some people said this to boost my spirits. Others said it to end a conversation. I was strong and therefore didn't need any help.

Yes, I am strong, but like all bereaved people, I also have weak times. I was never sure how I would feel. My feelings were hard to predict.

After Helen died, friends stopped by to offer their condolences. One rang the doorbell late in the afternoon, a time when my energy was dwindling. She stayed for more than an hour. Though she was a kind, caring person (and still is), I was exhausted and could hardly wait for her to leave. Accepting and answering condolences was hard for me. The urge to be alone was another issue.

Being alone, even if it was only for an hour, gave me time to think. Trying to answer "Why?" and "Why me?" questions was a waste of time. I stopped searching for answers and focused on being alive. I remembered the times I shared with loved ones. Instead of torturing myself and trying to answer unanswerable questions, I focused on the strengths of my loved ones. Helen was a wonderful mother. She was brilliant, a composite engineer with six special certifications, an MBA, and artistic talent. In addition, she had special certifications for industry. Before she died, she supervised three factory production lines. The company manufactured generators for American soldiers in Afghanistan.

"We're not making toasters here," she'd joked to her workers. "We're making generators, and we're on a deadline."

When my father-in-law died that same weekend, he was almost ninety-nine years old. He had met Dr. William Mayo (Will) and Dr. Charles Mayo (Charlie), the brothers who had founded Mayo Clinic. My father-in-law had enjoyed a long and successful career as a specialist in diseases of the chest. He was one of the finest people I'd ever known—thoughtful, funny, and wise. "Take credit for what you do," he'd advised. I followed his advice.

Walking to Sunshine

After Helen died, her former husband offered to move in with the twins and care for them until they finished high school. I was surprised because he and Helen had gone through a bitter, painful divorce. Life was changing quickly, and I wondered if I could keep up with the changes. The twins and their father lived in the house Helen had bought, and things seemed to be going well. Still, the twins needed us desperately after their father died. We were determined to be loving, caring, and protective grandparents. But sometimes I felt like I was walking through a dark forest and couldn't find my way. To help me see a path forward I read some of Earl Grollman's books. Would they help me emerge into the sunshine?

Rabbi Earl Grollman, a wise and prolific grief author, was a source of hope. I was familiar with his work and blessed to meet him when John and I were in Boston for a college reunion. We took Earl and his wife out to lunch. He gave me several of his books, and I treasure them. When my latest book came out, I sent him a copy. He called to thank me. "You can really write!" he exclaimed. I thought about his comment when writing went well and when it didn't. Earl gave me a verbal gift that day, something to treasure for the rest of my life.

Creating an Emotional Compass

Accepting the pain of multiple losses was tough. I thought about my feelings, especially the pain of multiple losses. Maybe I needed an emotional compass, a concept that came from Martha Beck, author of *Finding Your Own North Star*. Beck thinks there are four magic questions on one's compass:

What am I feeling?

Why do I feel this way?

What will it take to make me happy?

What's the best way to get what I want?[2]

Creating an emotional compass helped me move forward on the healing path. To do this, I went with the pain. I cried in the car. I cried in the grocery store. I cried in Target. I cried in the shower. How I cried. Crying was like a release valve on a pressure cooker. After every crying session, I felt relieved, thought more clearly, and was able to remember an article I had just read.

I needed to create new relationships with my deceased family members. These relationships depended on several factors: their characteristics, my characteristics, and any unfinished business we had. Some people did this quickly. Not me. Creating new relationships with deceased loved ones took several years. The process included both happy and sad memories.

Grief experts say the first step toward recovery is acceptance. While I agreed with this idea, the pain of the traumatic loss of my daughter was almost beyond words.

Experiencing grief was like the children's game of hide-and-seek. Grief hid for weeks or months, then jumped out unexpectedly and yelled "Boo!" I was determined to look grief in the face. We'd have a stare-down, and I refused to flinch away from it. Looking grief in the face required determination and resolve. I had both.

Even if I faltered or became exhausted, I refused to give up on myself. Step by step, I walked forward on my healing path. To be sure, some of the steps were baby steps, and I wondered if they were too small to count. Then I decided the size of my steps didn't matter as long as I was making progress.

Beck's book helped immensely. As she notes, I could choose to

---

2 Martha Beck, *Finding Your Own North Star: Claiming the Life You Were Meant to Live* (New York: MJF Books, 2001), 139–168.

be the star of my autobiography rather than the victim. This was a powerful idea and one I followed. In the process, grief brain became another point on my compass, and it scared me silly.

Chapter 2

Grief Brain: How Do You Lose an Egg?

Grief made me do odd things that were so troubling I thought I was going crazy. "The Egg Story," as I now call it, is an example of odd behavior. Several months after Helen died, I was getting ready for an hour-and-a-half drive to the Twin Cities for a meeting. I wanted to have extra protein for breakfast so I wouldn't arrive hungry.

I took an egg out of the refrigerator, set it down, and went to get the frying pan. When I reached for the egg, it was gone.

"It has to be here somewhere," I said.

A full day awaited me, and I didn't have time for nonsense. Who the heck loses an egg? I looked on the kitchen counters. No egg. I looked for a yellow splat on the floor. No egg. I looked under the kitchen island. No egg. *Hmm.* I was running out of places to look. There was only more place—the kitchen desk— and I found the egg. *Eureka!*

The egg was tucked underneath some letters. I didn't just lose an egg—I *hid* an egg. I wondered if the egg was a metaphor for grief. Did my subconscious want to hide grief? Was my subconscious telling grief to go away? Clearly, my mind wasn't working right when I lost the egg. *Sigh.* There was a reason for my behavior: grief brain.

What is Grief Brain?

Grief brain, also called "grief fog" and "widow's brain," is used to describe the normal confusion and forgetfulness of grief. *Normal* is the important word here. It's normal to be confused, forgetful, and stressed after a loved one dies. It's also normal to feel this way after a beloved friend or pet dies.

I read about grief brain, and as I learned more, I realized that I had experienced it after each loved one's death in 2007. When John died in 2020, I thought my previous experiences with grief brain would make this episode easier. But each episode of grief brain was different, and the common denominator was forgetfulness. My list of crazy, quirky mistakes seemed to get longer by the day.

I walked into a room and forgot why I was there.

I read magazine articles and remembered nothing about them.

I lost my comb and found it in the refrigerator next to the milk.

I dropped two of my treasured blue-and-white dishes.

I forgot how to increase the volume on my car radio.

I didn't know how to charge my mini vacuum.

I wrote checks incorrectly and had to write them again.

I lost my car keys, even when I vowed not to lose them.

These mistakes were upsetting. Bursting into tears without warning was always a shock. The crazy grief brain stuff kept happening. I forgot my computer pin number, the one I'd been using for years. I forgot the names of close friends. I could see their faces in my mind and tell you their favorite flavor of ice cream, but I couldn't remember their names.

At the rate I was going, I feared I would forget my own name. These events were upsetting because I thought I was functioning well. Sure, I'd made a few mistakes, but after all, I was only human.

Symptoms of Grief Brain

Experiencing grief brain was like walking around in a fog. My brain fog was so dense I could barely function. I learned more about the symptoms and effects of grief brain. The books and articles I read described me. Of all the symptoms of grief, weight gain and loss, real or imaginary pains, and exhaustion may be the most dramatic. These symptoms were in addition to age-related health problems. I was getting older, and sometimes I felt like I was 110 years old, a phrase my mother had often used.

Feeling down, another symptom of grief, was discouraging. If my down feelings continued for months, I knew they could become depression, and that would be a lot for anyone to handle.

Grief brain is a normal response to grief, but many bereaved people have never heard of it. I wasn't strange, I was normal, and I kept saying the word "normal" to myself.

But I wished someone had told me about what to expect from grief brain. In 2021, a year after John died, I experienced mental lapses. However, I didn't dwell on them or ever tell my relatives about them. I didn't want them to know an intelligent family member had lost an egg. (Now you know. Don't tell.)

My grief brain lasted about eight months, which was normal. Grief brain lasting longer than that could be problematic. Though I was prepared for John's death, and he died peacefully, my grief brain packed a wallop. My mental confusion worried me, and I wondered if my brain would ever return to normal. What would happen to me if my brain never functioned normally again?

A friend of mine became terribly confused after his wife died. He lost things, couldn't make decisions, dressed oddly, and had trouble speaking. The struggle to retrieve words from memory was so intense that my friend had to bow his head.

"Give me a minute," he said in a pleading voice. "Just give me a minute."

I waited patiently for several minutes. My friend couldn't find the words he desperately sought. He sighed, shook his head in disappointment, and opened his eyes.

"I give up," he declared, resting his hands on his knees.

I could tell giving up was hard on him, but my friend's embarrassment was harder. Grief brain was a monkey wrench thrown into my friend's life. And mine.

Grief brain threw me off-balance. I was usually an efficient person, someone who looked ahead, anticipated events, made plans, and always made lists. (List-making may be a genetic trait.) I certainly didn't plan for my mind to be muddled and useless. The mental confusion of grief brain shocked me, and I worried about doing something stupid.

A Recovering Brain

Recovering from grief brain was a start-and-stop process. Was I going crazy? Many bereaved people ask themselves this question. I thought I might be going crazy for several reasons. Crying was the first one on the list. Some days I cried almost constantly and feared I'd never stop. Crying bouts prevented me from doing all of my daily tasks, and that was upsetting.

Memory problems also worried me. Had my brain chemistry changed or developed a short circuit? I even wondered if I had a brain tumor. These were scary ideas, and I faced them alone. The year 2020 ended without John, and the New Year began without him. I was scared, but I kept my feelings to myself. However, if my memory problems became worse, I vowed to make an appointment with my primary care physician.

Trying to keep pace with these feelings drained my energy. Having low energy made coping with grief brain more difficult. I was used to accomplishing a lot in a day. Friends knew this, but I didn't.

"Harriet, you realize we live our lives at a different pace than most people," a friend said. "It's our normal pace." Her comment surprised me.

I never thought about the pace of my life until my friend pointed it out to me. Grief brain made me wonder if my energy, and the pace of my life, would return. Keeping up with the book business required energy, and my energy had almost disappeared. If my energy never returned, would I be the same person? Would I become a sloth and a stranger to myself?

Grief Brain vs. Alzheimer's

I worried about my mental capacity and that I was developing Alzheimer's disease. Even though I'd passed the mini mental status exam several times, I worried about how I would score on a detailed exam. Several wrong answers could change my score markedly. This worry led to more research. While memory loss and grief brain have similar symptoms, the duration of each is different.

Grief brain is a *temporary* response to crisis and comes on quickly. The response to grief hit me the instant my husband died. My mind jumped around from the present, to the past, to the future. I weighed options and searched for solutions. Doing this was difficult because my brain was constantly distracted. I knew my brain was working slowly, very s-l-o-w-l-y. Eight months later, once my brain processed the tragic news and accepted it, my grief brain went away. I was relieved.

Alzheimer's disease is *permanent* memory loss and tends to come on slowly. The body's main computer—the brain—is shutting down. The rate of decline varies from person to person. Older adults usually develop Alzheimer's, but it can also affect young people. Doctors, researchers, and drug companies have developed medications to slow the progression of Alzheimer's.

These medications help the patient and family members "buy" time.

This planning period changes the life of the patient with Alzheimer's, as well as the lives of family members and extended family members. Clearly, there are many options to consider: home care or a memory care facility, location of the facility, state regulations, staff training, activity programs, and staff-to-patient ratio. The last factor may be the most important.

Eight months before his health failed, John had developed memory problems. He recognized his memory lapses and chided himself. Though I was glad we lived in a retirement community that had a continuum of care, I didn't want to face the fact that John was close to needing this care. I didn't want to say "end-of-life care" out loud.

Grief Brain vs. Dementia

It's possible to have both dementia and grief brain. At least, that was my mother's experience. Mom had vascular dementia (ministrokes), and each one damaged her brain. At that time, health care professionals didn't know these strokes continued to spread. Though she was never diagnosed with Alzheimer's, her doctor said Mom's symptoms and behavior were consistent with the disease.

After my father died in 1982, my mother made some poor decisions. A confident person, Mom thought she was acting wisely, but she reacted irrationally when she decided to move to Florida to be near her sister. Without telling anyone, Mom called a moving company, arranged to have her furniture shipped, boarded a plane, and flew to Melbourne.

Later, her minister told me, "Your mother left everything she knew behind—her church, her friends, her neighbors, and her garden."

Mom and her sister saw each other a lot until my aunt Barbara became ill. I was visiting Mom in Melbourne at the time and drove her to the hospital to see her sister.

"You've got to get out of here, Barbara!" my mother said to her. I could tell Aunt Barbara wasn't going to "get out of here," and she died several days later.

Her sister's death affected Mom's memory, and after phone conversations and visits, we convinced Mom to move to Rochester to be near family. She lived in a retirement community and liked her studio apartment.

Mom grieved for her sister for months, and as her dementia worsened, she forgot her sister had died.

"I wonder what Barbara is doing today," she said several times. Mom's comment was really a question. I told Mom her sister had died, and she was shocked every time. The sad news was always new news, and Mom was shocked every time I said this. Mom shook her head in disbelief and cried.

For a day or two, Mom showed signs of grief brain, but then it left. Grief brain and memory loss made Mom so confused that she barely spoke. Watching Mom's behavior, and seeing her grieve for her sister, was torture. Poor Mom. Poor me.

Mom couldn't express her feelings with words, so I could only imagine how she felt. But I knew she was a prisoner of her own mind. Her dementia became so bad her physician transferred her to the nursing care wing of the retirement community. Each week, a volunteer reader came in and read to the residents.

"I can't tell you what the story is about," Mom admitted, "but it's very exciting."

Mom's mind continued to fail and, about a year before she died, I thought it was wise to get her power of attorney. She agreed to it and was willing to talk to our lawyer. Still, I thought she might balk at the last minute and ask me to cancel the appointment. If that happened, it would be a setback for my caregiving and a threat to Mom's well-being.

I called our lawyer and expressed my concerns. He understood my feelings and reassured me.

"People with memory loss can still deceive others," he explained. "They may do well in court and remember enough to convince the judge they are sharp."

He went on to say that he had handled many cases like this before and was good at it. Thanks to the lawyer's experience, my mother readily signed the POA document.

Mom's brain gave out, and she died quietly at the age of ninety-three. Her death made me a motherless child.

The Evolution of Forgetfulness

Forgetfulness, a major symptom of grief brain, evolved over centuries. As humans adapted, our brains adapted and changed. When we feel threatened, the brain goes into survival mode and decides whether to fight, take flight, or freeze. My brain went into fight mode. I refused to let grief brain take over my life.

I didn't lose any more eggs or put my comb in the refrigerator, but I broke more dishes. I almost made an expensive mistake. Though I didn't realize it, I'd put the electronic key for my car in my jeans pocket. When I went to wash the jeans, I found the key. Thank goodness! Replacing the electronic key would have cost me several hundred dollars.

Grief's Physical Effects on the Brain

Much like a sieve filters out bits, pieces, and lumps, grief brain filters out painful memories and feelings. Still, traumatic loss sparks feelings, memories, and angst. According to the American Brain Foundation, grief either strengthens or weakens the connections between nerves. This depends on the type of loss, how long it lasts, and the person's responses to it. If nerves are repeatedly weakened, the brain goes into default mode. This changes the cortisone level in the brain. Cortisone is a stress hormone, and we all have it. Too much cortisone generates extra stress.[3]

I didn't know anything about my cortisone level, but knew I was stressed to the max. I found ways to de-stress, and they worked. Slowly, day by day, the symptoms of grief brain faded. In some ways, I was grateful for grief brain because it was a normal, defensive response to death.

"Goodbye, grief brain," I muttered to myself. "I don't have time for you anymore. There's work to be done."

Loneliness and Collective Grief

Saying these words and thinking about grief work were indications of my brain returning to normal. Though I started to feel like myself again, I was lonely. John and I should be together in our apartment. He should be sitting in his wheelchair, reading the *Wall Street Journal*, and watching television. He should be asking me what we are having for dinner. He should be telling me about the book he is reading. He should be sharing stories about his life.

None of this happened and never would. I was alone.

Loneliness is a pervasive, corrosive emotion. There are many words for loneliness, including "lost," "defeated," and "depressed," but I felt hollow. The idea of eating alone was so painful I couldn't do it. I'm embarrassed to say this, but I ate standing up in the kitchen. Putting food on a plate was a rarity. Most of the time, I ate food directly from the skillet or the can.

---

3 "Healing Your Brain After Loss: How Grief Rewires the Brain," American Brain Foundation, September 29, 2021, https://www.americanbrainfoundation. org/how-tragedy-affects-the-brain/.

After I felt brave, I decided to try to eat at the dinner table, and it went well. Eating alone wasn't as terrible as I thought it would be. The pain of eating alone faded gradually, but I became sad when I looked at the rim of the table. John's wheelchair hit the rim many times and dented it. I felt the dents with my hands and cried. How would I survive without him?

Watching the news on television wasn't a happy experience. Every time I turned it on, there were stories about strife, famous people and others who had COVID-19, countries in conflict, drive-by shootings, school shootings, and natural disasters. In self-defense, I limited my viewing of news to once a day. When I watched the news, I felt connected to people I never met. Yet I felt I knew them. Grief experts call this "collective grief," or sadness that's felt by many people. You and I can come up with the names of famous people who died.

Betty White is an example. The "Golden Girl" was a television actress, movie actress, comedian, and devoted animal lover. Fans were happy when Betty celebrated her ninetieth birthday and hoped she would live to be a hundred. In preparation for Betty's historic birthday, the media prepared stories about her. Two weeks before her hundredth birthday, Betty White died. I admired Betty's spunk and philosophy of life. Thousands of fans like me grieved for her.

Collective grief is more than just sadness. It's an emotional connection to strangers who live miles or even countries away. Losing one famous person after another is a struggle for many. What is the effect of these losses on our culture? Researchers don't know the answer to this question yet.

Coping With the Down Days

The year after John died my grief brain was at its peak. I wanted to give my brain a rest, but I couldn't do that. There were dozens of tasks on my to-do list, and progress ranged from slow to nil. Recovering from grief brain was a slow process that came in spurts. I never slipped into classical depression, thank goodness. My brain struggled to adapt to the loss of my beloved John and the onset of more grief. I often felt "down" and wondered if I really was getting depressed.

Clinical depression is a mental disorder that gets worse over time. This depression can get so bad that the person becomes nonfunctional. If I didn't take some proactive steps to counter grief brain, my mind could turn to "squash rot," the term my brother-in-law had used to describe mental decline. I wanted to avoid squash rot. What steps could I take?

It took months to answer this question. Some solutions were simple, yet when they were combined with others, the results were surprisingly effective. Even if I only took one baby step, I was moving forward.

I didn't slip into classical depression after John died. Thank goodness. But I had "situational depression," a response to a traumatic or stressful experience. John and I had discussed situational depression after Helen died, so I already knew about it. As time passed after John's death, my sad, dour feelings eased and finally went away. I helped myself by eating right, getting enough sleep, writing, and talking with other widows.

I'm a visual learner, so marking the calendar with checkmarks helped me. I checked off the days when I had grief brain. In the beginning, most calendar squares were checked off. As the weeks passed, fewer squares were checked off. When I turned the calendar to the next month, no squares were checked off. I was encouraged because I could see my progress clearly.

Writing reminders on sticky notes helped me. I stuck notes everywhere—on the computer screen, the refrigerator door, the kitchen counter, and the bathroom mirror. It's a wonder I didn't stick a note on my nose! Some experts don't recommend sticky notes because they can get lost. The notes were clues to my day, and I didn't lose any.

I considered keeping a grief brain log, but I didn't do it. My books and articles served as my log. A diary and a log are different. You make daily entries in a diary, which can be a lot of work. You make regular entries in a log, which is less work. Entries may be weekly, every other week, or every two weeks—whatever works best.

Importance of Self-Care

Self-care became a priority. I divided large goals into smaller ones. Daily plans were shortened. For example, instead of buying groceries for the week, I bought groceries for a few days. Eating right was a given, and I tried to eat balanced meals. Though I sometimes had cereal or pudding for dinner, most of my meals were balanced. I drank more water and monitored my snacks.

Getting enough sleep was helpful. Seven hours per night was my goal. To reach this goal, I turned off the television an hour before I went to bed. I bought new pillows, a new duvet, and lowered the temperature in my apartment. I avoided eating spicy food for dinner. Even though my sleep was interrupted by bathroom breaks, I averaged seven hours a night.

Adding physical activity to the day was helpful. I walked more and tried to walk outside. A short walk helped clear my brain and find solutions to my problems. I enjoyed the fresh air, watching people, and watching birds. When it snowed or rained, I walked the aisles of a grocery store four times. The short walks made me feel better.

One time, an employee at the grocery store watched me go by, go by, and go by again. She looked concerned and asked, "Can I help you?"

I pointed to my pedometer and told her I was getting my daily exercise. She smiled.

Practicing self-kindness was essential. I injured my right hand and wore a brace for ten days, as per my doctor's orders. I couldn't type, which was frustrating to say the least. I ate with my left hand, missed my mouth, and spilled food on my clothes. I couldn't make the bed, which drove me nuts. To avoid seeing my messy bed, I closed my bedroom door.

Diaphragm breathing was helpful. Some people do diaphragm breathing while they're lying down. I did it while sitting or standing. Before I started, I calmed myself by closing my eyes and imagining a blank television screen, the one you see when the power fails. I focused on the image of a blank screen.

I then placed my hand on my upper chest and my other hand under my rib cage. I took a deep breath through my nose, held it for a few seconds, then blew it out with pursed lips. (I pretended I was a kissing fish.) When I did this, my stomach moved outward. Diaphragm breathing became part of my life. I do it before I give talks, workshops, and when I'm stressed.

I also tried counted breathing, an idea recommended by many grief experts. To do this, I counted my inhaled breaths and counted my exhaled breaths. Counting to four or five worked best. I rested for a minute between counted breaths. Counting my breaths diverted my mind for a few minutes, and this allowed my mind to rest. I wasn't completely focused on grief because I was too busy counting.

Counted breathing and diaphragm breathing helped me take control of grief brain. After doing these exercises, I felt more alert.

When I hear the advice, "Just breathe," I smile. Breathing is automatic, so of course I'm going to breathe. I wasn't going to hold my breath until my face got red, I felt faint, and keeled over. Each time I counted my breaths, however, I was more aware of the miracle of life. My loved ones would want me to be happy, and to do this, I tried new things and made new plans.

Grief Heart

Checking for "grief heart" also helped me. Grief heart, which is also called "broken heart syndrome" and "stress cardiomyopathy," is a response to the stress of grief. People who have grief heart feel like they are having a heart attack. Because I have a pig valve in my heart and two other leaking valves, I worried about heart attack and grief heart. These worries made my grief worse.

I also worried because I had bouts of atrial fibrillation. I had a special blood test, and it proved I didn't have a heart attack. What a relief. My stress level dropped and my enjoyment of life increased.

Women respond differently to heart attacks. To be on the safe side, I posted the symptoms of a heart attack for women on my bulletin board. As scary as the symptoms sounded, I knew grief heart was a temporary condition.

Treatment begins with lowering stress. This is done with medication, support groups, physical activity, and in some cases, a prescribed tranquilizer. The physician or nurse practitioner may prescribe medicine to lower blood pressure, regulate heart beats, and reduce fluid from the body.

Making Big Decisions While Grieving

Because of my grief symptoms, I postponed big decisions for six months. These decisions included buying "iffy" stock, making major purchases such as a new car, and responding to appealing ads online. I didn't want to repeat my next-door neighbor's mistake, one I remembered from childhood.

I was in fifth grade when our neighbor (Mom's best friend and my second mother) decided to get married shortly after her husband died. Mom had tried to talk her out of this decision, but her plea fell on deaf ears. Our neighbor got married anyway. A week later, she came home without her husband and never talked about him again. Despite gentle prodding and shared coffee klatches, Mom never learned the story behind the story.

This memory has stayed with me all my life, and I have learned from my neighbor's experience. I've resisted making any life-changing decisions while experiencing grief brain. It is better to be safe than sorry.

Another example of making major decisions while grieving happened in 2010 when John and I went to a university reunion. We saw many friends there, including a recent widow. She told us she was going to move out of her house and buy a new house in a different city. This was a major financial decision, and friends tried to dissuade her, including us. Our friend stuck with her decision.

"I know what I'm doing," she declared firmly, "and I'm moving."

After that, nobody said another word to her about her decision. Still, John and I worried about her. This grief brain story has a better ending. My friend bought the house she wanted and lived there for years with family members. Grief brain didn't get the best of her. When I think about the chance she took, I think my friend was lucky.

Creativity

Grief brain was a marker in my journey. I thought about the power of grief brain and wondered if it would stifle my creativity. Ever since I was in grade school and made books for friends, creativity was part of me. John often said he fell in love with my brain and enjoyed watching it in action. As I grew older, I realized creative minds worked differently.

This realization helped me understand the workings of my own mind. Art was an innate part of me. I couldn't look at anything without thinking about art: bright colors, muted colors, straight lines, spiral lines, repetitive patterns, bold lettering, and wispy lettering.

I've always been as interested in writing as I am in art and am always on the lookout for book ideas. I love words and have favorite ones. I love the rhythm of words when they are strung together. When I am in the writing zone, I am engrossed and less aware of what is going on around me. The older I've grown, the more I've accepted the fact that my mind is wired differently.

Even if you don't think of yourself as a creative person, working on creative projects can be healing. These projects can reduce stress when you do them alone or with others: a knitting club, jewelry-making workshop, or watercolor classes. Creative projects help to reduce our stress. Less stress enables us to enjoy life more. We become more aware of others, the changing seasons, and the beauty of our colorful world.

Chapter 3

Types of Grief

I have learned about many different types of grief. Like making good soup, grief has a lot of ingredients and requires patience, and I am patient with myself.

A few types of grief are anticipatory grief, traumatic loss, prolonged loss, primary loss, secondary loss, and ambiguous loss. I studied grief, wrote about it, and spoke about it. When I thought about my grief experiences, I imagined bumper cars at an amusement park. It was an odd image yet an apt one. The bumper cars represented different kinds of grief, and I was bumped time and again. Each bump was harsh, powerful, and painful.

I wanted to avoid grief and steer around it, but I couldn't.

My first experience with grief was when I was in fifth grade and our family dog died. My second experience with grief was when I was seventeen and my grandmother died. She had debilitating arthritis and lived with my parents and me. Grandma's bedroom was a few feet away from mine, and I would hear her moaning in pain at night. The pain became so severe that Grandma was taken to the hospital by ambulance. She was there for a few days and died.

Suddenly, grief became personal, and it scared me. At the time I didn't understand death, was afraid of it, and didn't want to attend Grandma's memorial service.

"You don't have to go," my mother said, and she meant it. My mother and father never commented on my absence.

Early Anticipatory Grief

Grief hit me again in 1968 on the day John received Air Force orders to Vietnam. This time I experienced anticipatory grief, a feeling of loss before a death or dreaded event occurs. While anticipatory grief doesn't have the shock factor of sudden death, it exacts the same terrible toll.

Edward Myers, author of *When Parents Die,* described the toll. "If a sudden death hits like an explosion, knocking you flat, then a slow decline [anticipatory grief] arrives more like a glacier, massive and unstoppable, grinding you down."[4] Anticipatory grief ground me down day by day. I felt a clashing combination of feelings I didn't understand.

One by one, I marked off the days on the calendar until John was due to leave. Every day was stressful, and as the months passed, my stress increased. Coping with stress and caring for two daughters was exhausting. I didn't understand my feelings. At the time, I didn't know about anticipatory grief, its symptoms, or its power. Now I do. Anticipatory grief can be life changing.

The dreaded day came. John flew to San Francisco, stayed overnight with friends, and flew to Vietnam. His orders said he was supposed to go to a base in Biên Hòa, and I sent letters and parcels to him there. Instead, John was assigned to Pleiku in the Northern Highlands.

I wrote to him almost every day. Well before Christmas, I sent him a white fruitcake with almonds. While the cake was still warm, I drizzled rum over the top. The letters and fruitcake were sent to the wrong address and sat in a holding center for several weeks. By this time, the news was old, and the fruitcake was boozy.

---

4 Edward Myers, *When Parents Die: A Guide for Adults* (New York: Penguin Publishing Group, 1997) 83.

John enjoyed the letters and ate the fruitcake.

I sent another Christmas gift to John, a photograph of me and the girls. The portrait was taken by a professional photographer. I wore one of my favorite dresses, a red dress with flowers. The girls also wore dresses and looked adorable. John was thrilled with his gift. Years later, he told me that he cried every time he looked at the photo.

John was appointed as commander of the base hospital and supervised its construction. He wrote to me regularly and taped messages for the kids. Our daughters were two and four-and-a-half years old at the time. Even though they were young, they missed their daddy. We listened to John's taped messages together. The girls couldn't understand how they could hear Daddy's voice and not see him. Hearing John's voice made me miss him more.

Acute Anticipatory Grief

Every morning when I got out of bed, I wondered if it would be *the day*. Would an Air Force officer, with a pained expression on his face, ring the doorbell and tell me John had been killed? I worried about this constantly. American soldiers were being tortured, and I prayed John wouldn't be one of them. The girls and I said grace before dinner and ended with the words, "God bless our dear daddy."

John sent the girls a cuckoo clock from Vietnam. I hung it on the wall next to the dining room table, where we could see it often. The girls loved when the door opened and the bird popped out, opened its mouth, and said "cuckoo." We could see the bird's red throat when it opened its mouth. To hear extra strikes, the girls pulled a chain on the clock. We heard countless cuckoos.

The Montagnards were one of about a dozen native tribes in Vietnam. The chief gave John a brass protection bracelet to let tribe members and members of other tribes know that John was to be protected. When Vietcong soldiers were near, John received advanced notice. He wore the bracelet every day. On the way home from Vietnam, John called me from San Francisco to tell me when his flight would arrive in Houston.

"Are you wearing the bracelet?" I asked worriedly.

"Yes, it's still on my wrist," he answered.

"I think it works. Keep it on!" I exclaimed. "Don't take it off until you walk in the door!"

John being in a war zone taught me about the power of anticipatory grief. Since then, I have experienced anticipatory grief many times, researched it, and began to understand it. The symptoms of anticipatory grief cast a wide net.

Focus on past, present, and future—I lived it.

Uncompleted loss—I lived it.

Emotional limbo—I lived it.

Time factor—I lived it.

Ongoing suspense and fear—I lived it.

Complexity—I lived it.

Sorrow tempered with hope—I lived it.

Thankfully, neighbors looked out for me and were extremely kind. When a hurricane was forecast for Houston, neighbors taped the patio doors and staked down the tree in the front yard. Another neighbor fixed my plumbing problem and offered to babysit. Their kindness helped me but didn't reduce my anxiety. Anticipatory grief followed me like a black cloud.

I couldn't escape anticipatory grief, no matter what I did or how fast I ran. Would my anticipatory grief ever end? Could I survive such intense feelings? Every day was a day of uncompleted loss, yet I couldn't falter. Two little girls depended on me. I had to be strong; I had to be their rock. Some days I felt like anticipatory grief was tearing me apart. When I felt discouraged, seeing my daughters' faces gave me the courage I needed.

But my stress continued to build. I'm ashamed to admit this, but one time I yanked my younger daughter out of the tub during bath time. She was having a tantrum, and I couldn't take any more screaming. I was ashamed of myself. I bundled my precious daughter in a towel, picked her up, sat in a rocking chair, and sobbed. This experience alerted me to the dangers of stress and fatigue.

Suspense and fear became part of my life. Because I didn't think others would understand, I kept my feelings to myself. Grief experts call this "stuffing feelings." I was stuffed emotionally but not physically. Though I cooked balanced meals for us and ate normal servings, I kept losing weight and dropped to ninety-eight pounds. The term "skin and bones" described me.

Before John left, I accepted a part-time job at an Episcopal school. I loved teaching and taught three mornings a week, just enough to divert my mind. The principal, teachers, and supportive staff knew John was in Vietnam. After my students left for the day, the custodian swept my classroom. We had a friendly relationship, and he asked how I was doing.

"I don't think I'm going to make it," I replied honestly. The custodian stopped sweeping, rested his hands on the broom handle, and looked at me intently.

"Mrs. Hodgson," he said in a Texas drawl, "you're gonna make it 'cause you gotta make it."

"Thank you," I replied softly and tried not to cry.

The custodian's words were a wake-up call. I *could* make it. I *would* make it.

Decades have passed since then, and while I don't remember the custodian's name or face, I remember his words. More importantly, I believed them. The custodian changed my life. His resolve became my resolve.

How Anticipatory Grief May Help

I think the most unique symptom of anticipatory grief is feeling sorrow and hope at the same time. When John was in Vietnam, I told myself he would come home safely. As my mother's memory failed, I told myself new medications would be invented to slow her dementia. When John's health was failing, I told myself modern medicine would save him. I experienced more episodes of anticipatory grief and realized it could be helpful—an idea that shocked me.

Anticipatory grief helped me see what was important and what wasn't. Everything was relative. For example, I hit a cement post and damaged the rear left fender of my car. A dented fender was nothing when compared to life. Gravy spots on a new blouse were nothing when compared to life. A clogged kitchen sink was nothing compared to life.

Anticipatory grief allowed me to rehearse my emotions, and I became better at identifying them. When a negative feeling came to mind—disappointment, fear, confusion, anger, and others—I named it immediately. I countered each negative feeling with a positive one. This took lots of practice, but I managed to do it, and I still use this technique.

Anticipatory grief gave me time to improve things. I wrote more letters to John's parents and my parents. I socialized with neighbors and friends. I purchased a book about crewel embroidery, taught myself how to do it, drew a picture of shells on canvas, and embroidered it. As always, my hands needed to be busy, and I kept them busy.

Anticipatory grief gave me time to review my life: what I did well, what I didn't do, and what I hoped to do in the future. This review was necessary if I was to keep moving forward on my healing path. Reviewing my life also gave me time to assess past and current feelings. Some feelings were more painful than others. I tracked them by keeping a one-word journal of my feelings. Before I went to bed, I thought about the feelings I had experienced that day and chose the words that described them best: *Okay. Down. Upbeat. Funny. Creative. Hopeful.* When I remembered to do it or wasn't too tired, I wrote the words on a calendar. If I didn't write the word, I imprinted it in my mind.

Traumatic Loss

In 2007, the traumatic loss of my daughter became imprinted in my mind forever. A traumatic loss is sudden, unexpected, and happens without warning. The loss of Helen was more than traumatic; it was violent. I pictured the crashed car in my mind and Helen's crushed, bleeding body. The images were torturous.

Her death was nature's mistake, an out-of-turn death. The car crash happened on a snowy February night. Helen and her daughter, one of the twins, were on their way home from a Girl Scout meeting several towns away. It was snowing, and the country road she was driving on connected to the highway at an angle. Helen turned onto the highway, didn't see the oncoming car, and was hit broadside. The Mayo One helicopter came to her rescue, and my granddaughter went to the hospital by ambulance.

A helicopter crew member called me. "Your daughter has been in a car crash," she said. "Her injuries are really bad, and your granddaughter probably has a concussion."

Oh my God.

The news sparked unease and fear. Earlier that evening when John and I were eating dinner, I had suddenly felt so nauseated that I didn't finish my food. This happened around six thirty in the evening. Was this the time of the crash? Do mothers have the same communication as twins? Had Helen thought of me on impact?

I never learned the time of the accident or the answers to these questions, and I had to make peace with that. Many of life's questions have no answers. A television news crew showed up at the crash site. The footage they took appeared on the early news. A friend called to warn me. "Don't watch the news tonight," she urged. "It shows your daughter's crash, and you don't need to see that." I thanked her for calling and followed her advice.

I didn't need to store these images in my conscious or subconscious mind.

Surgeons operated on Helen for twenty hours, but her injuries were so extensive the doctors couldn't save her life.

"We fixed one thing and had to fix another," the lead surgeon explained. I could tell by his facial expression and body language that he was truly sorry to share this news. He said he tested our daughter, and she was brain-dead. Our hopes for a miracle were dashed.

Helen was an organ donor. A representative from an organ donation organization came to the hospital. I wouldn't be able to do this woman's job, and I admired her courage. However, I wasn't pleased with her clothes. She wore a low-cut dress that was so out of place I wondered if she had come from a cocktail party. John and I sat down at a table with her to sign legal documents. Every time she leaned over, I saw her breasts and said a mental *oops*.

The "oops" happened several times. What an odd experience. John's brother and his wife came to the ER to support us, and they saw the woman's breasts. I felt birth and death were sacred experiences. The woman's revealing dress desecrated Helen's death. When family members talk about this experience, we refer to the woman as Mrs. Cleavage. She will always be Mrs. Cleavage to us.

John and my surviving daughter went to the police impound lot to see the damaged car. There was a lot of blood in the car, enough to fill an empty coffee cup. My surviving daughter, a licensed family therapist, has been shaken by the experience ever since. When John was an Air Force flight surgeon, he investigated several crashes and was used to doing this.

John didn't say much about Helen's crash and said nothing about her car. Helen's organs saved three lives and restored another person's sight. The organization sent remembrance medallions to the twins and an invitation to the yearly banquet. The twins didn't want medallions or a fancy dinner; they wanted their mother. The organization continued to send us invitations. Receiving them was so painful, that I asked for our names to be removed from the mailing list. This decision sounded harsh, even to me, but I couldn't handle any more invitations.

The traumatic loss of Helen was difficult to process. First, there was debilitating shock and disbelief. When I learned more details about the crash, Helen's death was even more traumatic. When she was barely conscious, apparently Helen had patted her daughter on the knee to comfort her, a maternal thing to do.

Prolonged Loss

I watched my own mother cope with prolonged loss over the death of her sister. At the time, I was in my fifties, and, despite life experience and caregiving skills, prolonged loss was a trying experience for both of us. Prolonged loss, sometimes called prolonged loss disorder, happens when a bereaved person's grief lasts longer than normal grief. This type of grief is hard on the bereaved person and family members.

Though Mom lived in a retirement community, I did something with her, or for her, every day. Mondays were errand days. Tuesdays were bill-paying days. Wednesdays were out-to-lunch days. Fridays were shopping days. Saturdays or Sundays, Mom came to our house and I cooked gourmet meals. When necessary, I washed Mom's clothes and mended them.

None of these efforts slowed her relentless mental decline. Mom would dial my phone number but didn't recognize my voice. She would call three times in a row, I answered, and then she would hang up.

"I keep calling and you're never home," she declared angrily. Mom's decline had an impact on my physical and emotional health.

My mother died when I was in my late fifties, and I realized I was exhausted. Some might say Mom died of old age, but I thought differently. The brain is the body's main computer, and Mom's brain gave out. It took a year for me to regain my energy and feel like myself. The process was a journey of its own. I lapsed into backward thinking. Had I helped Mom as much as I could? Did I unknowingly hurt her?

I thought about a conversation we had when Mom was angry about something. "I'm doing my best," I said defensively.

"You may be doing your best, but it isn't good enough," she countered.

I was hurt by her words. I couldn't believe Mom was dissatisfied after all the time and effort and money I'd spent on caregiving. Then I realized Mom was right. My caregiving wasn't enough to make her young again. My caregiving couldn't erase the symptoms of dementia and diabetes. My caregiving couldn't make her happy.

Primary Losses and Secondary Losses

Years later, when John died, grief hit me again. Losing John was a primary loss, the death of an immediate family member.

Secondary losses are the areas in your life that have been affected by your primary loss. My secondary losses hit like a bulldozer.

I kept a list of secondary losses, and as the months passed, it grew longer and longer. I was shocked every time I added something to the list.

Lack of companionship was a secondary loss. Two people no longer slept in our four-poster bed, ate meals together, discussed books, went out for dinner, or mingled at events. Two people no longer laughed together and looked at each other with love. Widowhood was a lonely place. Now there was just me, and I didn't know if I could make it on my own.

Less joy was a secondary loss.

I didn't think joy was true joy unless it was shared, and I wanted to share happy experiences with John. But I couldn't tell him about my new position as an assistant editor, or my most recent published books, or about writing *Winning*. These were painful, in-your-face realizations. John was my champion, someone who believed in me, encouraged me, and always had my back. Now he was gone.

Though I was able to feel joy, it didn't have the sparkle it once had. This was hurtful. I wanted to share happy feelings with others, so I shared them with friends, people I barely knew, and strangers. If the mail truck slowed down, I'd probably share my feelings with the mail person. In my mind, sharing upbeat feelings made them authentic and real.

Reduced income was a secondary loss.

Prior to his death, John had received retirement checks from the US Air Force and 3M (Minnesota Mining and Manufacturing). I still receive checks, but they are far less. This worried me. When our financial adviser called to update me on my account, I told him I felt guilty about buying underwear and art supplies. There was a slight pause in our conversation.

of miles to get there. When my friend arrived, she was shocked by the behavior of family members. Instead of welcoming her, family members ignored her. Several family members turned and walked away.

"I thought I'd be asked to say a few words of remembrance," she explained. "I felt invisible."

My friend was physically present but felt invisible because no one acknowledged her loss. For my friend, being unnoticed was another loss, painful and unwarranted. Did she experience a different form of physically present loss? Since I wasn't sure of my answer to this question, I emailed Dr. Boss. She replied immediately, and her answer was affirmative.

Physically absent loss pertains to heart-wrenching events when you don't know whether your loved one is alive or dead. Runaway kids, kidnapping, soldiers in combat, explosions, bridge collapses, and natural disasters such as tornadoes, floods, mudslides, and earthquakes are all examples of when one experiences physically absent loss. John lived through an earthquake, a scary experience he remembered for the rest of his life.

John was four years old when his family moved to Lima, Peru, and they'd lived there for five years. He had learned Spanish quickly and spoke it like a native, according to his parents.

Lima was generally a safe place, but there were earthquakes—something John's family wished they hadn't learned. As soon as the ground began to shake, John's father went to the hospital where he worked while his mother asked friends of the family to care for John and his brother.

"I didn't know if my parents were dead or alive," John recalled. "My brother and I were staying with nice people, but we didn't really know them." John's experience is an example of ambiguous, physically absent loss. Every bereaved person has their own style of grieving. I called myself a "direct" griever, someone who identified problems quickly and searched for solutions. In the long run, being a direct griever saved me time. Other bereaved people may slip into avoidance and do everything they can to avoid grief. Avoidance works for a while until it doesn't.

Acceptance Leads to Healing

When I accepted the reality of loss, I took a giant step forward. This was a logical step because I'm a nonfiction writer. Reality was, and continues to be, my business. The acceptance of reality was a life changer to be sure, and it helped me believe in the future. I began to plan the future I wanted and made a list of goals. Since many goals involved writing books and getting them published, I made a budget to facilitate my goals.

As much as I wanted it to happen, not every day was a day of acceptance. Sometimes I faltered and experienced the blues or temporary funk—feelings of discouragement that were obstacles to my goals. *Darn it*. If the pain became unbearable, I redirected my thoughts and remembered my loved ones' achievements. I spent lots of time thinking about my daughter, Helen, mother of twins, composite engineer, MBA degree, production manager with six industry certifications, and community volunteer. Her achievements were impressive, and I was glad she lived long enough to enjoy them.

Taking a Break from Grief

Taking a break from grief was another forward step.

In July of 2007—five months after Helen died—John, the twins, and I seemed to be existing rather than living. Maybe it was time to do something different. On impulse, I suggested a family trip to Alaska. The twins were excited about the idea, so I made the arrangements. Going to Alaska was the change we needed. We rode a train over mountains, swooned over mixed berry pie, and saw a moose and other unusual things.

The trip benefited all of us. We interacted with one another, swapped stories, smiled more often, and though grief was always in the back of our minds, enjoyed a much-needed break from sorrow. Everyone felt better when we returned home. Taking a break from grief was a healing step, and I took others. Taking these steps was satisfying and I was proud of myself.

I took a break from grief.

I worked hard on acceptance.

I identified my grieving style.

I continued to learn about grief.

I tallied my secondary losses.

I watched for different types of grief.

I found something to smile about each day.

Because I was so busy with two teenagers, the months passed quickly. The twins graduated from high school with honors and college with high honors. John and I moved out of the townhome we lived in for five years and into Charter House, a retirement community owned and operated by Mayo Clinic in Rochester, Minnesota. Things were going well until COVID-19 hit and changed everything.

Chapter 4

The Only Person on the Planet: COVID Days

Being isolated during COVID-19 made me feel like the only person on the planet. The loneliness of COVID-19 is one of worry and sorrow. It affects the body, mind, and spirit. My loneliness was so strong I felt like a soldier conscripted into an army I didn't want to join. Being a conscientious objector wasn't a possibility. Forward was the way to go. How could I cope with loneliness? Would I survive it intact? Answering these questions was difficult. As I searched for answers, I tried to practice self-kindness.

Some answers, like continuing my hobbies, were comforting. Other answers, like the rapid spread of COVID-19, were terrifying. I had scarlet fever when I was a child and our house was quarantined, but I'd never experienced a pandemic.

COVID-19 scared me to the marrow of my bones. I live in the Midwest and thought the pandemic might not reach Rochester, Minnesota—an unrealistic, delusional idea.

Olmsted County, in the southeastern part of the state, had one of the highest infection rates in Minnesota. I was frightened before and doubly frightened after I read stories about Mayo Clinic employees who had the virus. This put a strain on both the staff and patients. I worried about health care personnel who worked regular and extra hours. A person can only work for so long.

John and I were already stressed. John's health was failing and would eventually need a continuum of care, so we moved out of our townhome and into a retirement community called Charter House. Adjusting to community living at Charter House was slower than we anticipated and took more than a year. While we had a good reason to move, we wondered if we had moved into Charter House too soon. We were happy living there, but not extremely happy.

We missed our townhome. I'd spent months planning and decorating the 1,700-square-foot home and making it wheelchair accessible. The townhome had wood flooring and a wheelchair-friendly shower. A horticulturalist had planned the front, side, and back gardens. Everything had turned out just as planned, and we'd lived in the townhome for five years, and they were almost idyllic.

There wasn't room for garden space around Charter House, so management brought nature inside. The apartment building was filled with giant green and flowering plants. Gardening committee members created artistic flower arrangements and changed them often. While I appreciated these things, it wasn't the same as having a garden.

When I walked out of my apartment, I didn't connect with nature. Instead, I was greeted by a long, carpeted hallway, and this was discouraging. I missed our colorful garden: pink petunias, giant red geraniums, and black-eyed Susan plants. We'd put two free-standing bird feeders in the backyard. A variety of birds came to the feeders: sparrows, juncos, finches, goldfinches, nuthatches, red-winged blackbirds, cardinals, and even crows.

Smart as they are, crows were not my favorite birds. When I yelled, "Go away, crows!" and waved my arms to scare them, the birds never flinched. They flew to nearby trees, waited until I went back inside, then returned to the feeders. My loud voice wasn't a match for scheming crows. The crow scenario happened many times. Being outsmarted by crows was a blow to my ego.

John and I settled into our Charter House apartment and felt safe until the pandemic reached Rochester. The virus blew into town like strong winds from the Dakotas. We only left the apartment for medical appointments. Though I occasionally went shopping (yes, I wore a mask), most of our groceries were ordered online. Isolation was a new experience for us, and we didn't like it.

Charter House went into prevention mode. Visitors had to sign in at the front door, answer questions, and wear stickers. Residents were vaccinated and received booster shots. We had to wear masks properly—over the nose and mouth—everywhere we went. Four masked people were allowed in an elevator at the same time. Yellow tape marked where we should stand, and a sign asked us to limit conversation.

All common areas were closed—the dining room, exercise room, library, movie room, and fireplace room—until further notice. Social activities were canceled. Special events (pianists, choral groups, popcorn day) were canceled. The Mayo Clinic wellness center was also closed. John and I understood these measures, but they changed our lives.

We felt like we were living in a cocoon.

Some residents had previously walked every floor of the building for exercise. They were now asked to stay on their own floors. Other residents walked in the parking ramp—not a safe decision. Wellness center staff came to different floors and led exercises. According to the grapevine (which could be wrong), a few residents did yoga in their apartments. Some exercise was better than none.

Charter House did everything it could to help residents. Mail was delivered to our door. Free coffee was delivered to our door.

Take-out meals were delivered for free. Holiday candy, wine, and cheese were delivered for free. I asked the delivery people about their jobs and was astonished to learn many were managers.

"I don't mind doing this," one said cheerfully. "At least I have a job." The weekly newsletter reminded residents to wear masks properly, practice social distancing, watch for symptoms, and wash hands frequently. Residents who ventured out of their apartments were asked to wash their hands after they returned.

Hand sanitizer was available everywhere I looked: by the elevators, in the laundry room, in the hallways, in public bathrooms, and in the lobby. Mayo Clinic installed thousands of sanitizers in its buildings. I sanitized my hands so much they became cracked and raw. Lotion didn't help; my hands remained chapped, and they finally healed in June.

A COVID Scare

While being together was a blessing, the absence of social contact made us feel alone. We read books and articles, discussed them, and had vibrant conversations. Humor had always been part of our marriage, and we laughed together. John "got" my humor and I "got" his. We told stories and told the same stories again. Laughter brightened every day.

But COVID-19 wasn't a joke and catching it could jeopardize our health. I checked on John and he checked on me. One day we felt so sick we thought we had the virus. Interestingly, we had many of the same symptoms. Though he didn't say it at the time, John thought he was going to die. He asked me to call 911.

"Really?" I asked.

"Yes," he replied. "Do it now." I called the number. An ambulance holds only one person, so I ordered two. John and I went to the emergency room department in "his" and "her" vehicles. Such togetherness.

We were both tested for COVID-19 and the results were negative. Follow-up tests showed that John had advanced prostate cancer and that it had spread to other parts of his body. I had cellulitis, a skin condition that could be fatal. I was treated with antibiotics and dismissed two days before John. I felt bad about leaving him alone at the hospital. Though I was glad to be home, I worried about John constantly. His health was fragile, and I knew challenging days were ahead.

Getting Help

Every day, agency caregivers came to help get John up and dressed. Some days, especially in the winter, the caregiver was a no-show. Several times, the agency called and told me the caregiver for the day had slid off the road into a ditch. Sorry as I was to hear the news, it put me in a bind, and I had to get John up by myself. This kept happening, and I was exhausted. Clearly, I needed some more help and searched online for it. I also asked Charter House residents if they knew of any nurses who could care for John.

I took my name off the agency list and hired a retired registered nurse (RN). She was cheerful, intelligent, experienced, and giving. John enjoyed her immensely. The nurse became a friend and remained a friend after John died.

COVID-19 wore on and wore us down. Only essential health care workers were allowed in the building. I had to prove that John's physical therapist and RN were essential to his health. I called the therapist and nurse and explained the situation. They agreed John's health would deteriorate without their care. Administrators approved the nurse and physical therapist.

Life became somewhat normal, but I developed a new health problem: a constant sore back. My back had been bothering me for months and was getting worse. I ached when I walked, when

I helped John stand, when I sat down, and when I slept. A painful back often awakened me from sleep.

Finally, I told John about my backache. "I wanted you to know," I concluded. "I don't think I'll be able to do this much longer." In other words, my caregiving days were limited. John looked at me intently but didn't reply.

Weeks passed. My backache became worse, and John's health deteriorated. After John came home from the hospital, he tried to use the standing frame and couldn't. His legs failed, and I felt like I'd failed him. At that moment, I realized I didn't have the strength to lift John; my strength had run out. The timing couldn't have been worse.

"I can't do this anymore," I announced.

Did I just say that? The words echoed in my mind, and I wished I could retract them. I looked at John and saw a calm expression on his face. He knew what was happening. A Home Health nurse was on hand that day, and she called for help. Two aides arrived quickly, transferred John to a gurney, and wheeled him away. This happened so fast I was shocked.

When the time came for John to move to nursing care, I wanted the transition to be gentle. I wanted to discuss the pros and cons with him. I wanted to tell him I would always be close by. Everything I wanted to avoid happened anyway, and John's transfer was sudden and abrupt. I felt guilty about the way the transfer happened, and I'm not good at handling guilt.

John was his usual strong, stoic self. Gifts aren't always wrapped in fancy paper. Moving to nursing care without complaint was John's gift to me. I cried after he was wheeled away. Feelings had been building up for weeks, and I felt like a geyser waiting to erupt. I knew the beginning of the end had come. So did John.

Supportive Care

He had a double room, but no other patient was ever assigned to the room. This gave John more storage space. The room had a ceiling lift—something John needed—and large windows. When I looked out the windows, I saw a roof. Not the best view, but a source of light and sunshine. A television was mounted to the wall across from John's hospital bed. Before he moved to nursing care, John had started to get forgetful. His long-term memory was excellent, but his short-term memory was fragile. Moving made John more forgetful, and he asked the same questions. He called every day to check on me. Though he usually dialed the number, as his memory loss increased, aides had to dial it for him. Knowing John, I'm sure asking for help was difficult.

During one of our conversations, John asked where I was living. He thought I lived in a different building. "I live in our apartment," I explained. "You're on the third floor, and I'm on the eighteenth floor. We're in the same building." There was a pause in conversation while John processed this news.

We were near, yet far apart.

John struggled to find the words he sought, but I understood him. Our conversations were short and meaningful. "I love you to eternity," he said.

"I love you the same way," I replied.

How much time did John have left? I promised myself that John wouldn't die alone. Despite the promise, I wondered if I had the strength to witness the end of his life. Still, I tried to be positive. John's love had been a source of strength when he was in Vietnam and when I faced health challenges. His love would give me the strength I needed.

Anticipatory grief sapped my energy. Long-term anticipatory grief was worse. I felt like I was walking through a dark rainstorm, pelted by feelings and the unknown. I wanted to cry but suppressed my tears. If I cried, I knew I wouldn't stop for hours. More than any other time of life, John needed a loving, supportive wife, and I tried to be that person. I would not fail him.

Finding Positives

Always a list-maker, I jotted down positive thoughts about John moving to nursing care. The positives didn't outweigh the negatives or change John's rapidly failing health. However, seeing these points on paper made me feel better. I was able to see some positives, and this is what I wrote:

John is safe and receiving good care.
Gathering information early is better than later.
We are still a team.
Anticipatory grief could shorten my post-death grief.
Alerting our financial adviser is a smart thing to do.
Putting assets in my name makes sense.
John will have a peaceful, pain-free death.

John's health deteriorated, and he called more often. He knew the end was near and requested an update on our finances several times.

"I've never worried about you and money," he said.

His words were reassuring and boosted my confidence. Years ago, I supervised the construction of three houses. If I could do that, I could manage finances alone.

"Do you have any symptoms of COVID?" John asked.

"Not one," I answered.

"I'm glad," he responded.

"I'm glad too," I agreed.

The phone was quiet for a few seconds.

"How will you get along?" John asked. He was asking how I thought I would get along without him. John was looking out for me.

"I will be okay, honey," I replied gently. "Okay" wasn't the best word choice, but it was the only word I could think of—a word that covered many scenarios. My reply seemed to comfort him, and I wanted to do that. I wanted his life to end peacefully and without worry.

In sixty-three years of marriage, our personalities had merged and our love continued to grow. As stressed and sad as I was, I loved John more than ever.

"You are part of my soul," I shared, "and I am part of yours." John didn't comment. I think he was processing my words.

When Death is Near

In hindsight, I realized John's behavior was normal for someone who was paraplegic. His behavior changed nine months later and indicated that death was near. I had missed all the signs. John lost his appetite and ate as much food as a two-year-old. Instead of lunch, John wanted ice cream, and I gave it to him. While he was eating, John often closed his eyes. He became quieter and often had a faraway look in his eyes.

John was always cold, so I boosted the thermostat. Extra sweaters and blankets didn't warm him. Getting enough sleep was increasingly difficult. John watched late-night television, something I didn't know. He turned on the television as soon as I finished with his bedtime routine. The television was always too loud.

"Please turn it down, honey," I implored. "I don't want to be a grumpy caregiver tomorrow."

After being awake all night, John would take short naps

during the day. Even though John was in pain, he kept this news from me. Finally, he admitted his pain.

"I'm in pain all the time and try to ignore it," he said matter-of-factly.

Maybe I was in denial, but I had attributed John's behavior changes to poor sleep and medication changes.

I should have known.

I wished I'd known, but I didn't.

If I'd known the signs of death, I would have been a better caregiver. This information would have helped me cope with John's behavior changes and plan for living alone. I think physicians, nurse practitioners, nurses, and social workers should share this information with family members. These wouldn't be cheerful conversations, but they would be helpful, honest conversations.

I visited John the day before he passed. I pulled a chair next to his wheelchair and read the paper for a while. John answered my questions, though he never opened his eyes. His replies became shorter and shorter. John seemed to be in another world. I gave him a quick kiss on the cheek and told him I was going back to our apartment.

"You're sleepy," I said. "Maybe you need a nap."

"I've already had a nap," John replied. "I'll take another." That was our last conversation.

When I was getting ready for bed, a nurse called to say the end was near. I grabbed a sweater, put it on over my pajamas, and rushed to be with John. On the way I prayed for strength. Would I have the strength I needed? I called my daughter, and she arrived two hours later. A kind nurse brought us coffee and snacks, but we hardly touched them.

"He can still hear you," another nurse confided.

I didn't doubt that John could hear me, but I wondered if he understood what we were saying. My daughter and I stood next to John's bed and talked to him most of the night. She thanked her father for all the things he had done for her. I kept saying, "I'm here, honey."

Nurses came in at regular intervals and turned John over to prevent bed sores. They also adjusted his oxygen flow. All night, John hovered between life and death. I went from being an emotional wreck to being resigned. At eight in the morning, I realized I had forgotten to take my heart medication.

I rushed back to the apartment, brushed my teeth, took my meds, and returned quickly. I was too late. John had died a few minutes after I left. Though I wasn't with John when he died, my daughter was with him, and we had kept our promise. John didn't die alone. The role I dreaded for months—widow—was now mine.

That night, I returned to the apartment and thought about our marriage, our daughters, and all the years we shared. I'd been up all night, but I wasn't sleepy, and my mind was racing. My thoughts were so jumbled I felt like I was watching a movie. The movie wasn't an account of my own life but someone else's life portrayed by actors. John's death seemed unreal. I couldn't accept it. Maybe tomorrow. Maybe next week. Maybe next month, but not now.

The Effects of COVID-19

The spread of COVID-19 added to my feelings of loneliness. Television news programs reported on mounting fatalities. At first, I thought the statistics were in thousands only to find the numbers were in the millions. No city or state was immune. Businesses closed. Public and private schools closed. Parks and movie theaters closed. Parents were forced to homeschool their children.

The school closures had one positive outcome. Parents realized that teaching was a difficult, demanding, and tiring job. While some parents rallied to fill the school gap, other parents were in a quandary.

"Teachers should be paid a million dollars a year," a mother posted on Facebook. Her idea was supportive, impractical, and impossible.

COVID-19 and its variants continued to spread. As a former teacher with twelve years of classroom experience, I had an idea of what was coming, and my instincts were correct.

Many children were harmed by the lack of a school routine, contact with peers, contact with teachers, and after-school activities. If a reporter held a microphone to my face, I'd say kids were lonely. Television and print journalists referred to homeschooled kids as the "COVID Generation," an apt term. The term excluded parents who had chosen to homeschool their kids and organizations that supported this type of learning.

America's children proved to be COVID kids. Scores on competency tests dropped markedly. Team sports faltered due to lack of practice. Parents turned to online courses for support. These courses didn't replace the daily school routine or socialization. Years from now, I think authors will still be writing about the deadly virus that changed families, our nation, and the world.

Just Me, Alone

Life became lonelier. I sorted through John's clothes alone, crying the whole time, and donated them to Goodwill. John's physical therapist delivered the clothes for me, which was extraordinarily kind and helpful. I managed our finances alone, and it wasn't fun. I arranged for car repairs alone, though I didn't know about cars or speak car-talk. I cooked meals (some pretty sparce) and ate alone. I attended social events alone. Alone. Alone. Alone.

I slept poorly in the four-poster bed we had shared for decades. I missed snuggling up to John when I was cold, seeking comfort after a bad dream, or simply because I loved him. I didn't dress carefully because John wouldn't see me. I didn't look forward to life's little things—baking cookies for John and drinking coffee together. Without John, half of me was gone.

I was empty.

Online Memorial Service

I wrote John's obituary alone. Fortunately, I'd kept a file about John's careers as a specialist in aviation and aerospace medicine; his time spent in the Air Force and then at NASA, Houston; and his career at Mayo Clinic. Writing his obituary was a mental challenge. How could I select highlights from a life that was filled with them? I sat at the computer, tried to write, and burst into tears. This start-and-stop pattern repeated many times.

Finally, two days later, I was satisfied with what I had written. I sent John's obituary and photo to the newspaper. John never bragged about his accomplishments, so his obituary surprised some colleagues, friends, and relatives.

"I didn't know John did all those things," a relative commented. When I wrote John's obituary, I was surprised at all he had accomplished in his life.

The pandemic changed John's memorial service. Instead of an in-person service, it was online. Planning took months. I contacted a few family members and asked if they would be willing to make short videos about their memories of John. My daughter wrote a touching tribute to her father and described our marriage as "one for the ages."

I asked the minister when he would be available to lead the

service. I wanted John's service to be special and came up with an idea about hats.

Americans often say a person wears many hats. John wore many hats, and I selected four of them for his memorial service. The online program listed this segment as "Hats," which was short and to the point. I held up each hat and made a short comment about it.

I picked up a helmet with a large cross on it. "This is the hat John wore in Vietnam," I explained.

Then I picked up a helmet with an oxygen hose connection. "This was John's Air Force flight helmet, and it was custom-made for him."

Then I picked up a helmet with an insignia on it. "This was John's Air Force Colonel's hat."

Finally, I picked up John's tan corduroy cap. "This was John's family hat, his weekend hat," I said. "Of all the hats he wore, this was his favorite."

I sang a hymn for the service. Before the pianist arrived, I did some vocal exercises, but the hymn wasn't in a good key for my vocal range and I thought I'd "blow it." The hymn was "Just as Long as I Have Breath," words by Alicia S. Carpenter and music by Johann G. Ebeling.

I chose this hymn because of the line about saying yes to life. If I had to choose a line that described John, this was it. Again and again, John said "yes" to life. He had the courage I often lacked.

John was my talisman and my rock. If he watched the service from another realm, whatever that might be, I hoped John would be pleased with it. About three hundred people viewed the service—a tribute to John—and a life well led. Most of the comments I received were about John's hats.

The online service wasn't the same as an in-person service.

I couldn't see friends, chat with them, accept their hugs, or hug them back. Missing pieces like these made me feel more alone.

Talking to Myself

The service was online for a week and linked me to the outside world briefly. Then I was back to feeling alone. Reluctant as I am to admit this, I started talking to myself.

"Come on!" I yelled when the computer was slow.

"Good job," I said when I finished an article.

"You did it," I said when I submitted a manuscript.

"That was delicious," I said when I set down the fork on my plate.

"Stop talking to yourself," I said when I heard my voice.

Verbalizing my stream of consciousness was abnormal behavior. Maybe I'd finally gone "bonkers" and was incapable of lucid thought. So, instead of speaking aloud, I started whispering. I figured I wasn't technically talking aloud if I whispered. Whenever I started whispering, I stopped immediately.

A month or so later, my whispering ceased. I connected with more people via email, Facebook, and Twitter. Like the virtual service, however, these contacts weren't the same. I was left with me, myself, and I. Though I don't know this for sure, I think I looked and acted lonely. I didn't look energetic, that's for sure.

Construction sounds in my apartment building made me feel better. I have a caregiving personality, so when I heard the sounds, I had the urge to pick up a hammer and help. The sounds of hammering and buzzing machinery were proof of life. Other people were in the building and working. I wasn't the only person on the planet.

According to the Centers for Disease Control (CDC), loneliness is serious business. Loneliness isn't just social isolation.

A person can be with others and still feel lonely. I found some startling CDC statistics on loneliness.

Social isolation was associated with about a 50 percent increase in dementia. Loneliness was associated with a 29 percent increased risk of heart disease and a 32 percent risk of stroke. Loneliness causes a 68 percent increased risk of hospitalization, and a 57 percent increased risk of emergency department visits.[6] These numbers, and others, suggest loneliness can cause physical and emotional harm.

Anti-Loneliness Campaign

Loneliness was personal for me. We'd had Golden Retrievers for years and I missed them. One dog was named Sally and the other was named Max. I longed to have a pet again, but according to retirement community rules, I could only have fish. In my mind, fish weren't true pets; they didn't respond to names or offer affection. For centuries, dogs had adapted to humans and learned to "read" their body language and conversation.

While it was fun to see the pet therapy dogs that came to Charter House, they weren't my dogs. The dogs didn't know me, and I didn't know them. I wanted a dog and couldn't have one. This fact added to my loneliness.

Many of my friends had died, and I missed them. Their deaths made me think about my father-in-law. As the years marched on, more of his friends died, and he was the last one standing. If Dad was upset, he didn't show it. Dad would simply say, "Fred (or whatever the name was) was a wonderful person and I'll miss him." Then Dad went on with his life.

---

6 Loneliness and Social Isolation Linked to Serious Health Conditions," Centers for Disease Control and Prevention, April 29, 2021, https://www.cdc. gov/aging/publications/features/lonely-older-adults.html#print.

"You have enough money," he assured me. "The next time you feel this way, please call me." I promised to do this.

For many, downsizing is a secondary loss.

Family members may have to move to a smaller place to save money or be near grandchildren. Thankfully, I didn't have to move after John died because I was already home. I live in the apartment we shared and feel safe here. When the time comes—and it will—I have access to a continuum of care.

Living among people who understand this age and stage of life comforted me. These are just a few examples of my secondary losses, and there are dozens more. When I added my primary and secondary losses together, the total was long, and the impact was huge.

Ambiguous Loss

Ambiguous loss wasn't a direct part of my grief experience, but it affected friends of mine. To understand this type of grief, I read *Ambiguous Loss* by Dr. Pauline Boss. According to Boss, ambiguous loss is unacknowledged or unresolved grief. Because the loss is unclear, this type of loss is stressful and often tormenting. Boss divides ambiguous loss into two categories: physically present and physically absent.[5]

Physically present loss occurs when a person is physically present but psychologically absent, such as with Alzheimer's disease, drug addiction, or chronic mental illnesses. Physically absent loss occurs when you don't know if a loved one is deceased or alive. I didn't understand the categories until a friend told me about her sister's memorial service. My friend lived on the West Coast and the service was on the East Coast. She flew thousands

---

5 Pauline Boss, *Ambiguous Loss: Learning to Live with Unresolved Grief,* (Cambridge, MA: Harvard University Press, 2009) 5–9.

I didn't want to be the last person standing or become a CDC statistic, so I started an anti-loneliness campaign.

Step one: I joined an informal support group of residents. Our discussions were honest and funny. Laughing with them changed the day.

Step two: I took advantage of free coffee for residents. Getting coffee gave me opportunities to talk with friends, strangers, and staff. Even if I only said a few words, my loneliness was reduced. I lived with residents who understood loneliness and this time of life.

Step three: I talked with friends about loneliness. One friend had moved across the country to live at Charter House. She missed her husband, her house, and her friends. Another friend said they were lonely and didn't know what to do about it. Other friends thought loneliness was a serious topic that couldn't be explained. Despite their interesting careers, these friends talked the most about their husbands and children.

One friend lived alone and felt separated and lonely due to COVID-19. She had no contact with others, and the silence in her apartment was oppressive.

"Then the phone rang," she explained. "I said, 'Oh good. I have someone to talk to and am not alone.' " My friend looked forward to future phone calls.

Loneliness reminded me of a paper I wrote for Study Club about Robinson Crusoe. Daniel Defoe's novel, *Robinson Crusoe,* was published in 1719 and is considered one of the first English novels. Defoe's story is based on the real life of stranded sailor Alexander Selkirk.

In the novel, Robinson Crusoe is stranded on a Caribbean island for twenty-eight years. Selkirk was stranded for eight years, and during that time, he lost the ability to speak. He was miraculously rescued and returned to England. He had to learn how to speak all over again.

Was I a female Robinson Crusoe at risk for losing my ability to speak? In some ways, I had lost touch with reality. I walked into John's bedroom to tell him something and remembered he wasn't there. I thought about calling a friend and remembered they had died. My circle of friends was shrinking rapidly, and my loneliness was relentless.

I lost a future with my parents, my in-laws, my brother, Helen, and John. For the rest of my days, I'll wonder what my daughter would have accomplished if she had lived. What would we have done together? What holidays would we have celebrated? What would she think about the twins becoming adults? So many questions and so few answers.

When he was about sixty years old, I asked John to write his memoir, or dictate it. He never did. Maybe John didn't write it because he didn't realize he had an unusual life. Aerospace medicine, aviation medicine, internal medicine, preventive medicine, and Air Force service were ordinary things for John. Yet John's life was extraordinary and I was blessed to share it with him.

The deaths of family members and friends hit close to home. I realized I could die at any time. After our mother died, my brother said, "I'm in front now." I understood his comment.

When John died, I believed I was next in line to die. If I wanted to write more books, I'd better get cracking. If I wanted to put more effort into book marketing, this was the time to do it. If I wanted to do something unusual, now was the time. No sitting around and feeling sorry for myself. Having a pity party wouldn't be beneficial and would delay grief healing.

I asked other widows how they coped with the loss of their husbands. My next-door neighbor said she thought of her husband every day.

"You have to keep going," she said.

Like my neighbor, I think about John every day and miss him. I had many happy memories. As time passed, thinking about John became less painful.

The second year as a widow or widower is often called "the lonely year." It was a terribly lonely year for me. Remember when I said I was a list-maker? I wrote a bill of rights and gave copies to parents who belonged to the local chapter of the Compassionate Friends.

Because I'm Grieving . . .

I grieve in my own way and time.
I learn about grief brain and cope with it.
I say my loved one's name often.
I help others by sharing my story.
I let myself feel a wide range of feelings, many of them opposites.
I burst into tears without warning, and that's okay.
I wander off my healing path and return to it.
I give myself permission to make mistakes.
I ask for help even though it's difficult.
I promise to take good care of myself.
I draw upon familiar rituals and create new ones.
I find comfort in happy memories.
I turn to spirituality and faith for comfort.
I search for new meaning in life, including goals.
I give myself permission to laugh again.

There's a difference between loneliness and feeling alone. I have lived both. As a freelance writer for forty-five years, I've grown used to working alone for hours and enjoy it. Working at home doesn't make me lonely. The opposite is true. When I email other authors, I connect to a world of ideas. I have high standards and try to meet them.

"You work for a tough boss," John had often said.

"You're right," I agreed. "I'm a tough boss and can be hard on myself."

I did many things alone: get up and dressed, make the bed, fix meals, and pay bills. I'm not lonely when I do these things. The loneliness of grief was another story. Without John's presence, the silence in my apartment was unbearable. The only sounds I heard were the ticking of the antique clock and the television if I left it on.

Now John was gone. He didn't say, "Honey, is there more coffee?" or "This is delicious," or "I like your new sweater," or "I love you." I missed the sound of John's voice. I seemed to be stuck in loneliness and wanted to be unstuck.

New Motivation

Vicki Panagotacos would say I needed impetus. In her book *Gaining Traction*, which is about starting over after the death of a life partner, she writes that having courage helps us see the realities of life more clearly. "If you focus on having courage and being curious, you are imagining a positive reality as if it were happening right now."[7]

I tried to live mindfully and see the beauty in ordinary things. The sun shining on a building across the street. Iridescent raindrops sliding down my apartment windows. New buds on my African violets. A stray ladybug or two. Observations like these helped me live mindfully. My thoughts shifted from what I didn't want to what I wanted: new friends, new experiences, and happiness.

I ran into a stumbling block when I tried to make new friends.

---

7 Vicki Panagotacos, *Gaining Traction: Starting Over After the Death of Your Life Partner* (Steady Guide Press, 2014), 96.

Creative people don't easily switch from being alone to being social. If I wrote for hours, it would take me a half hour to be social again. Fortunately, I knew I was capable of this transition

and dusted off my coping skills. I could make new friends, be a friend, share my talents, and smile more often.

I gave workshops and speeches. I sent out a free monthly newsletter. I volunteered for several organizations. Bit by bit, I made progress in the friendship department. What other things could I do? This question stumped me until I came across *The Five Invitations* by Frank Ostaseski.

Ostaseski describes grief as a "secret teacher hiding in plain sight."[8] So true. Death is a natural part of life, and none of us get out of it alive. Developing an awareness of our everyday activities can help us awaken ourselves to life. Not facing the truth—the death of a loved one, friend, or colleague—leads to emotional pain. As he concludes, our lives are our lives, and we need to be present.[9]

My outlook was simple—nothing ventured, nothing gained. I often wanted to be alone and felt guilty for it. Friends tried to be helpful and invited me to dinner, and I would turn them down. To process John's death and the host of tasks that awaited me, I needed to be alone. I had calls to make, bills to pay, and documents to file. Purposeful alone time differed from feelings of loneliness.

Alone time helped me identify problems, work on solutions, and move forward on my healing path. Doing these things made a happy future seem possible.

When people asked about my alone times, I said, "I'm an

---

8 Frank Ostaseski, *The Five Invitations: Discovering What Death Can Teach Us About Living Fully* (New York: Flatiron Books, 2017), 1.

9 Ostaseski, *The Five Invitations*, 14.

interesting person." Sure, there were times when I was lonely, but they were short-lived. Besides, I was too busy to be lonely.

John O'Donohue describes loneliness in his poem, "For Loneliness," with the words "deep black hole." The dark hole has a blue flower in it with a mystical light "which will illuminate in you the glimmer of springtime."[10] O'Donohue's words inspired me and helped me see small details I had previously missed.
I found my flower, the mystical light, and the promise of spring. I was only able to do this, however, after I repaired the holes in my support system.

---

10 John O'Donohue, *To Bless the Space Between Us: A Book of Blessings* (New York: Doubleday, 2008), 128–129.

Twin grandchildren at high school graduation ceremony. *Photo by Kenneth Presley.*

Photo with twin grandchildren shortly after they moved in with us.
Photo by Haley Earley Photography.

Harriet at The Compassionate Friends National Conference in Houston, TX.
Photo by Amy Hodgson.

Family photo with twins and great grandchildren.
Photo by Haley Earley Photography.

Harriet and John. *Photo by Elizabeth Nida Obert.*

Harriet relaxing in her favorite chair. *Photo by Kathy Meyer, RN.*

Harriet with two of her recent books. *Photo by Kathy Meyer, RN.*

Daughter Amy with her beloved dog. *Photo by Vicki Nicole.*

Harriet in front of Charter House lobby art.
Photo by by Kathy Meyer, RN.

Chapter 5

Fixing Holes in My Support Hammock

My support system was frayed and had random holes, like a hammock left out in the sun for too long. The hammock could support me briefly, but not for long and not in an emergency. In fact, my support system could have given way at any moment. How had this happened? I felt guilty about letting my support system lapse. After all, I was an educated, independent woman with years of life experience who should have known better. I used to think building a support system was a choice, not a necessity, but life changed my mind. Repairing my worn support system was both a choice and a necessity.

To strengthen my support system, I needed to update it, and it was time for action. However, I ran into a problem. Grief had changed me. Friends, and those who had known me for years, didn't recognize the different me. They were bewildered and didn't understand my behavior. I couldn't blame them because I barely understood it myself. If I was aware of the changes, others were also aware, and the changes were shocking.

> I was more emotional about everything.
> I was unpredictable to them and to myself.
> I was confused and disoriented much of the time.
> I wasn't as much fun as I used to be.
> I didn't laugh often.
> I wasn't spontaneous anymore.

Updating my support system wasn't a sign of failure; it was a sign of self-care and respect. Even if I rarely used the support system, it would always be there, ready and waiting for me. I would have one less thing to worry about. Besides, there were benefits to having a system in place.

Types of Support

There are five kinds of support: individual, informal, formal, disease-specific, and health organizations. Individual support came from family members and close friends. Informal support included friends, acquaintances, and strangers. Formal support was a support group led by a qualified leader. Disease-specific support was available from local hospitals and church groups. Support from health organizations included those such as the American Heart Association.

Instead of using every type of available support, I chose the ones that would help most. I chose people who understood the depth of my grief. They didn't expect me to recover in a few weeks or say hurtful things like, "Aren't you over grief yet?" The names and organizations on my support system list were a lifeline. I grabbed these lifelines and held on tight.

As I beefed up my support system, I answered key questions. The vague answers disturbed me. Vague wouldn't cut it in times of crisis. These are the questions I asked myself and answered.

Are the contacts on my list current? *No.*
Is this a list of informed, reliable people? *I think so.*
Can I contact people/organizations quickly? *Maybe.*
What worked and what didn't? *I'm not sure.*
How can I update my support system? *Working on it.*

Updating my support system was a delayed response, and I wasn't proud of it. Don't make the mistake I did and wait too long to check your support system. Checking your system every six months is wise. I needed reminders, and you may need them too. Write "Check support system" on the calendar or put a sticky note on the refrigerator.

I imagined my support system as a series of ever-widening, concentric circles, with each circle serving a different purpose.

The grief I felt was mine, so I put myself in the center of the smallest circle. The next circle included support from a physician or a nurse practitioner. The next circle included religious and spiritual support from my church. The next circle included social support from friends and acquaintances. The fifth and final circle was support from local and national health organizations.

Once I determined these general categories, I searched for specifics. What names should be on my contact list? People of different ages were a must. An older person has wisdom a younger person hasn't yet developed. A younger person has fresh ideas and is technologically savvy. Of course, I didn't ask people how old they were and guessed instead.

Checking my support system was like taking photos from different angles; some pictures were blurry while others were clear. I typed a list of contact numbers and stuck it on my office bulletin board. I put another copy of the list on the refrigerator door where it could be seen.

My brother-in-law and sister-in-law lived in Wisconsin, but they remained on the list because they visited Rochester often. They were "keepers." I added new contacts to the list: my primary care physician, Charter House Home Health services, and the Charter House chaplain. These additions filled the gaps in my support system and strengthened it. What a relief.

My support system hammock started to look better.

Getting a Grief Buddy

I also thought outside of the box. A few weeks after John died, I came up with the idea of having a grief buddy. When I was having coffee in the corner shop, I met a recent widow, someone I knew but not very well. She was a long-term resident of Charter House and an outgoing, approachable person.

"I know your husband died a short while ago," I began. "Would you like to be my grief buddy? We could get through this awful time together."

"I'd love to be your grief buddy!" she exclaimed. And that was the beginning of our friendship.

We agreed on some buddy ground rules. One, we would meet at ten o'clock on Tuesdays. Two, we would meet in my apartment. Three, we could say anything and everything we wanted. Four, what we said was confidential. Five, if we couldn't meet, we would call. These rules were easy to follow.

Talking with someone who understood my feelings was such a relief. I didn't have to hide my feelings or worry about them. My friend understood, and I thought of her as my grief angel.

We met for several months. As the seasons changed, our meetings dwindled, became irregular, and finally ceased. The grief buddy idea had served its purpose. If we needed to talk to each other, my friend and I could always get together. The grief buddy door was always open.

The weekly meetings were a win-win for both of us. Months later, I met my friend in the lobby. She hugged me (we were wearing masks) and declared, "You changed my life!"

I tried not to cry. "And you changed mine," I replied.

We're still friends and laugh at each other's jokes. She laughs so hard at my stories that tears come to her eyes. Being with her is a joy, and I wished I'd met her sooner. I wished I'd met the Lobby Ladies sooner too, an outgoing, helpful, humorous group.

The Lobby Ladies

The Lobby Ladies, as we became known, were a group of eight or ten people. Every afternoon, we met in the fireplace room near the lobby. The name stuck after a member referred to us as the Lobby Ladies. I joined the group and realized it was an informal support group in disguise. Our meetings lasted about an hour.

The group operated on a come-when-you-can basis. Anyone could join our group; the more the merrier. Men were encouraged to join the group, and one did. Members of the group bonded quickly, and no one felt bad if a member had to leave early. Gossip wasn't on the agenda. We discussed kids, grandkids, news headlines, politics, committees, and illnesses.

If we hadn't seen a member for a day, we would check on them. We often ate in the dining room together. "Isn't it wonderful that we can talk like this?" one commented.

"This is my happy place," another added, and others agreed.

I wouldn't be as happy as I am today without the Lobby Ladies. Members waved me off when I left for Houston to speak at The Compassionate Friends National Conference in Houston, Texas, and welcomed me back when I returned.

"Tell us about your trip!" one exclaimed.

I told them about the conference, its purpose, my flight to Houston, and my workshops.

"Now, are you ready for this?" I asked.

Group members nodded.

"After I finished my workshops, I looked down and realized I was wearing mismatched shoes! I couldn't believe my eyes."

The Lobby Ladies (and one Lobby Lad) roared with laughter.

"Oh, Harriet, that is so funny!" a member said.

"Well, it was 4:45 in the morning when I got dressed, and I

was half-asleep," I added sheepishly. "The shoes were different styles, but they were both black, so I don't think anyone noticed my mistake."

Now group members check my shoes to see if they match. Though I was somewhat embarrassed about the shoe caper, I had a good belly laugh. Despite two college degrees, extra graduate courses, and certification, I'd worn mismatched shoes. Sheesh! The Lobby Ladies were, and continue to be, an informal support group and my dear friends.

Offering to Help

Others who heard my grief story weren't as understanding. "If you need anything, call me," was something I often heard. Independent people like me rarely call because we don't want to bother anyone. We tend to keep going and, but not always, find our way. However, I have accepted help when I was desperate, learned from this help, and the comments I received. Today when I offer help to a grieving person, I am very specific.

> *I'm going to the grocery store. Give me a list and I'll shop for you.*
> *Driving with me would be easier than driving alone. I'll pick you up at seven this evening. Is that okay?*
> *I called to tell you I'm delivering soup in an hour. It's frozen, and you can eat it whenever you want.*
> *I read a book that helped me and may help you. I'll leave it in your mailbox.*
> *I'm a good listener. Call me this afternoon and we'll talk.*

Joining a Support Group

Joining a support group can help those who are grieving. Many support groups were available in my area, and they differed widely. Before I joined a group, I did my homework and considered the following factors.

Type of group: Support groups are supposed to meet needs. They include faith-based groups, disease-specific groups, end-of-life groups, after-death groups, and more. I wanted to find a group that fit my needs.

The meeting place: Support groups meet in churches, hospitals, and places that have a minimal charge or are free. I looked for a group near my building to reduce driving time.

The meeting time: Because I get up around four thirty or five in the morning, I preferred to meet during the day. I don't like to drive at night, but I can if I need to.

Frequency of meetings: Many groups will meet on a weekly basis. I didn't have the time to meet more often. Once every two weeks didn't appeal to me.

Number of members: A small group suited me best. Before I joined a group, I needed to know how many members were in the group. Was the group accepting new members?

The group structure: I needed a group that was a true sharing, not a pity party. Group members would share coping tips, discuss the pros and cons, and come to conclusions.

A test drive: Before I joined a group, I decided to attend a few meetings. Instead of talking, I would just listen and observe group interaction.

Helpful leads: I wanted support group meetings to provide me with information about experts, organizations, and plans. It would be beneficial if the group had a resource library.

My feelings: After a meeting, I wanted to feel better. I knew from experience that I didn't need to be friends with all members to benefit from meetings. When someone spoke, I could learn from them and try their helpful tips.

If the support group didn't meet my needs, I could always drop out. A lack of confidentiality would be a reason to leave a group. I would also leave if the leader was abrupt or preachy. If I decided to leave, I would be courteous, respectful, and soft-spoken. I would follow John's advice: "Never burn your bridges."

Caregiving Support

Informal and formal support can be life changing. I looked for notices about support groups in newspapers and magazines. I used the search words "support groups" and "kinds of support groups" and found many listings.

After I became a GRG (grandparent raising grandchildren), I tried a direct approach. I'd called Social Services and asked if there was a support group for grandparents raising grandchildren.

"We used to have one," the representative said. "It disbanded a couple of months ago. That group is gone."

"Gone?" I asked in surprise. "But the number of grandparents raising grandchildren is going up by the day."

"I know, and I'm sorry," she said. "I don't know what happened, but the group is gone."

"Will the group start up again?" I asked.

"I don't know. I'm sorry," she concluded.

"Can you think of any alternatives?" I inquired.

"Not at the moment," she replied.

"Thanks for your help," I finished.

Our conversation was over. Though the call hadn't helped me, I thanked the woman for her time. I didn't understand why the support group was gone. There were dozens, if not hundreds, of grandparents raising grandchildren in the city of Rochester alone. They probably needed support, and I needed support. Maybe the GRGs were too tired to attend support meetings, lived too far away, or the meetings were held at inconvenient times. It was a mystery to me.

Years later, when I was John's caregiver, I joined a caregiving support group at my church. Meetings were held after the eleven o'clock service. A friend of mine, a certified grief counselor, was the group leader. She was a kind, gentle soul and an attentive listener. The meetings were helpful, but only about five people came to them. I was disappointed when the group eventually disbanded.

The Compassionate Friends

Joining a formal group worked for a while, so I decided to join Compassionate Friends (TCF), an international organization for those who have suffered the loss of a child. To this day, it has been the best group I ever joined.

TCF members include parents, grandparents, and siblings. There are TCF chapters across America and in other countries. Hugs, comfort, and laughter can be found at all local and national meetings. Author Mindy Corporan was a keynote speaker at the Compassionate Friends 2002 National Conference in Houston, Texas.

Corporan's father and son were murdered by someone who hated Jews. Audience members were spellbound by her tragic story. Mindy turned to friends for help and found it.

"I was very blessed to have my own circle," she admitted. She encouraged the eight hundred attendees to find their own circles and keep listening. "Our hearts tell us what to do."

I was glad I attended the conference, and I'm glad to be a member of the local TCF chapter. Attending chapter meetings gave me opportunities to meet other bereaved parents. Tissues were always within reach. Talking about my daughter's death eased the pressure of grief. TCF parents understood me, and I understood them. We were patient with each other, which was comforting.

Condolences

Attending TCF meetings made me think about my surviving younger daughter, who is a bereaved sibling. After her sister died, she wasn't prepared for all the condolences she received. People offered words of sympathy at church, the grocery store, or when she was walking the dog. While this was heartwarming, telling the story of her sister's death again and again was exhausting. All she heard was talk, talk, talk.

"So I went to the coffee shop where nobody knew me," she confided. She visited the shop so often that staff members knew her first name, but they didn't know her last name or her story. "That's why I kept going there," she shared. "It was the only relief I had." My daughter was grateful for those mini breaks.

The people who offered their condolences were trying to be helpful. In a way, these people were an informal support group. But every explanation my daughter gave drained her energy, and her energy was already low. My daughter needed to be alone. At a time when she needed peace, my daughter had no peace.

Author Earl Grollman calls alone times "five-minute vacations." I liked his description because five peaceful minutes could boost my spirits. According to Grollman, quiet times are necessary for respite, reprieve, and re-creation.

"There is healing in solitude," he explains.[11]

---

11 Earl A. Grollman, *When Your Loved One is Dying: A Compassionate and Comprehensive Guide for the Living* (Boston: Beacon Press, 1980), 105.

I understood his words, and as weeks passed, my daughter understood them too. Her coffee shop visits were five-minute vacations—a brief time away from grief.

Grief isn't right or wrong. It is personal.

Thanksgiving

Helen was born on Thanksgiving. While I was in labor, I smelled roasting turkey and seasoned dressing—my favorite part of holiday dinner. I wanted dinner even though I was in labor. Turkey dinner wasn't part of my delivery plan. Ever since she was born, we celebrated Helen's birthday on Thanksgiving.

My niece invited our family to Thanksgiving dinner the year after Helen died. She and her husband lived in a rural area with two goats, a cat, and a few chickens.

Dinner was fantastic, and the twins enjoyed petting the animals. This wasn't an ordinary Thanksgiving, but it was different and gave us a break from grief fatigue.

The solution of changing locations doesn't always work, but that time it did. It wasn't a normal holiday in terms of location or family members, but that was okay. We spent Thanksgiving with family members who loved us, and that is what mattered most. Our Thanksgiving was happier than anticipated. That day, family members were an informal support group.

Resources for Support

While joining a formal support group can also be helpful, things may not go as planned. This is the nature of support groups. Membership may be stable, or people may come and go. A group member may change jobs, move to another city or town, or develop a chronic illness. Changes like these alter group behavior, and members need to adjust to them.

Everyone who grieves, no matter how old they are, where their loved one died, or how they died, needs to share their feelings.

"You have to deal with the [emotional] flood," a friend explained.

John died from acute prostate cancer, heart disease, and lung disease. I had taken him to medical appointments, managed his medications, and arranged for outside caregivers. Caregiving was a consuming job, and I didn't have the time to check with national organizations or local chapters of these organizations. I just wanted to get through the day.

I searched for online support organizations and started with Mayo Clinic Connect. The website has dozens of support groups: cancer, kids and teens, caregivers, dementia, ear-nose-throat, heart-blood health, COVID-19, and more. I joined the grief group and continue to participate to this day. Group members posted painful stories, and they almost broke my heart.

I found other sources of support and felt good about having some choices. These resources may help you.

Grief counselors: Therapy for various types of depression.

What's Your Grief: Website and blog with articles about grief.

Open to Hope: Website dedicated to grief. Includes articles, television, podcasts, webinars, books.

Association for Death Education and Counseling (ADEC): Organization for professionals. Offers thanatology certification and hosts a yearly conference.

Light a Candle: Movement and website offering candle prayers for the deceased and articles about grief.

Center for Loss and Life Transition: National organization led by Dr. Alan Wolfelt. Provides books about grief and mourning, and offers training for a certification in Death & Grief Studies.

Grief Share: Resource to find recovery support groups in your area.

Grief Watch: Books, gifts, and resources for those who are grieving.

The Grief Toolbox: Website offering support groups, articles, DVDs, and other resources to cope with grief.

Grief in Common: Zoom support, individual coaching, learning "hub."

Grief Anonymous: Support group and magazine.

The Compassionate Friends: Nonprofit organization for bereaved parents, grandparents, and siblings. Hosts a yearly national conference.

Centering Corporation: Nonprofit company and online magazine that offers more than five hundred grief resources.

Before I became a regular website visitor, I tried to find out who owned it. I looked for membership fees. I looked at the authors' names and recognized some of them. I also checked the website's reputation. Was the site trying to help me, or was it just trying to sell me stuff? The answers to these questions helped me say yes or no to online support.

After-death support is available online and from local organizations. Rochester had several hospice organizations that provided end-of-life and after-death support. Some organizations had support groups and discussion groups for the bereaved.

Many national organizations—the Alzheimer's Association, American Heart Association, American Association of Retired Persons (AARP), and others—have local branches. National organizations could help me, but I didn't use them because I had been so busy with caregiving for John. I always had a long to-do list. The decision to not use national organizations was personally good for me.

What to Say and What Not to Say

Previously, I wrote about the things people had said to me. I ignored many of these statements and learned what *not* to say. Don't say any of these sentences to a grieving relative, friend, acquaintance, or stranger. All of them are hurtful, and if you're at a loss for words, it's better to say nothing.

God must have needed a child in heaven.

Everything happens for a reason.

You'll meet someone else.

Aren't you over it yet?

It's time for you to move on.

Your husband is in a better place.

Just get another dog.

None of these statements are helpful, and they may cause more harm than help. These statements sound crass, as if the speaker hasn't thought them through. How these words are spoken and where they are spoken can alter the meaning. From my view, condolences should never be given in haste. Here are some examples of what you could say to a grieving person:

I'm sincerely sorry for your loss.

You did everything you could.

Your husband was an amazing person.

You were a devoted caregiver.

How can I help you?

I would be glad to listen to your story.

Answers to "How are You?"

Answering the question "How are you?" always threw me off-balance. How did the person think I was after so much tragedy? Usually when someone asks this question, they expect one reply: "Fine." I used this answer at first to end painful conversations. But I wasn't fine, knew it, and came up with different answers to this common question.

Months passed, and my next answer to the question was, "Okay." I liked the answer because it was common language and fit many situations. "Getting along" was my third answer, the one I used in the middle stage of grief. This answer implied progress, which seemed to satisfy people.

When I felt stronger, I answered the question with one word: "Coping." I only used this answer with close friends.

Finally, well into my grief journey, I said "I'm good." And I was good because my support system began this journey with me. I had identified the gaps and fixed them.

To move forward on the healing path, I needed to become my own support system, a responsible person in charge of myself. My early efforts at creating a personal system were a false start—confusing and ambiguous. I wondered why.

In her book, *Loving Someone Who Has Dementia*, Dr. Pauline Boss writes, "It's up to you, in your own mind, to create a safe space—perhaps even a delicious place—where you know . . . that you have done your best and can do no more."[12]

These words resonated with me, and I took them to heart. I

---

12 Pauline Boss, *Loving Someone Who Has Dementia: How to Find Hope While Coping with Stress and Grief,* (New York: Wiley, 2011), 141–142.

felt I could help others who were grieving, not just relatives and caregivers of patients suffering from memory loss. Reaching out to others would help them and help me. What steps did I take?

I continued to learn about grief. While this wasn't fun reading, it helped me understand grief in general, types of grief, styles of grieving, what I was going through, and what others were going through. The more I read, the more my compassion grew, and I resisted judging myself. I practiced patience.

Permission to Laugh

I gave myself permission to laugh. Laughter released some of the tension I was feeling, and according to medical experts, it stimulates organs in the body. Since I was a child, I joked around and tried to leave a laugh behind. I also tried to "catch" laughs as they went by.

I went to Mayo Clinic for an ultrasound test. The instructions I received: change in dressing room two, put on a hospital gown, come out, lock the door, take the key from the lock, loop it on my wrist, and say I was ready. Just as I finished putting on the gown, someone knocked on the door. "Come in," I called.

"I can't come in," a woman chuckled. "The door is locked."

"Sorry," I replied. "That was an automatic response."

I unlocked the door, opened it, and saw a woman doubled over in laughter. "That was so funny!" she exclaimed. "You made my day."

"Well, if you came into my apartment, I'd give you coffee and cookies," I countered.

The woman laughed even harder. While she conducted the test efficiently, she continued to chuckle. "If I meet you again, I'm going to call you Mrs. Come-In," she said.

"Well, this is the face to look for," I replied, and lowered my COVID mask.

"I'll look for Mrs. Come-In," she repeated. "You really made my day."

Before the test, I felt sleepy. After the test, I felt energetic and upbeat. Laughter changed my outlook on the day. This is just one example of "catching" the laughs as they go by. I looked for laughter each day and found it. Every laugh eased my grief.

It took courage to laugh. At first, my ability to laugh was fragile and brief. Laughing became easier with practice, and I felt more like myself. Even a short "heh-heh" boosted my spirits. Some would say I was going with the flow. Katherine Ingram, author of *Grief Girl's Guide*, refers to changes like these as *flowing*.

She added this word to the flight, fight, or freeze responses. "Flowing is the fourth approach to grief and only one that will enable you to heal," she writes. She summarizes her idea with the words, "Flowing is growing."[13] How was my life flowing? Was I growing?

Back to Me

It took more than a year after John's passing when I began to feel stronger. I returned to volunteering, giving talks, and workshops. My friends thought I was doing too much. My reaction was totally different.

I felt like I'd come home.

At Charter House, I led a grief doodling workshop, and it was well received. The comments were positive. All the workshop attendees thanked me for giving it, but one comment stands out in my mind.

"Your workshop was helpful and entertaining," a woman

---

13 Katherine Ingram, *Grief Girl's Guide: How to Grieve, Why You Should, and What's In It for You* (Lodestone Press, 2020), 65.

began. "I'm going to keep doodling to cope with grief. It's better than throwing eggs at a wall."

"That sounds messy," I replied, "but thanks for coming."

After she left, I thought to myself, I'd never throw eggs at a wall because I'd have to clean up the mess, and that wouldn't be fun.

I shared my grief story at in-person conferences, online conferences, and in the books I wrote. Writing helped me clarify my thoughts, identify problems, and find solutions to them. Though I often wondered if I'd write another book (I don't know why I did that to myself), an idea would always come to mind and I would start writing. This became a life pattern.

When he was still alive, John always had faith in me and felt writing was an integral part of my soul. "You couldn't stop writing even if you wanted to," he commented.

John's instincts proved to be true. Another book was always waiting to surface in my mind.

When I felt down, as we all do, I thought about the benefits of having a support system. I became a more empathetic person, something I mentioned in a previous chapter. Though I became more compassionate, I confused it with empathy.

Empathy is the ability to feel another person's feelings and, perhaps, respond to them. Compassion is deep sympathy for someone else's misfortunes and the desire to help in some way. I had both feelings and helped others by writing and speaking.

The deaths of loved ones, relatives, and friends affect me in other ways. Looking back, I realize I am a kind person, as kind as my mother had been. In this troubled world, and in these troubled times, I feel more kindness is needed. I go out of my way to be kind to others and receive waves of kindness in return.

Learning about other grief authors, reading their work, attending support meetings, and local and national conferences linked me to other bereaved people. I wasn't alone. I was in the company of people who understood. No explanations or apologies were necessary. When I stumbled on my healing path, these people understood and were forgiving.

If I fell flat on my face, group members would understand. The formal and informal groups I interacted with were helpful, but none fit my role perfectly. Because I'd cared for three generations of family members, I understood the role.

I needed enough strength to finish the story—a course in Caregiving 101. How did I find this strength?

Chapter 6

Caring for You, Caring for Me

I used to think that raising grandkids was the biggest challenge of my life. No more. Caring for John at the end of his life was the biggest challenge. Around 2013, when we were still living in our Cape Cod house, a life-saving surgery for a dissected aorta caused John to be paraplegic. Becoming his caregiver was my new mission—a sacred mission—and I would do my best. Though I had cared for my mother and twin grandkids, I had never cared for someone who was paraplegic, and feared I wasn't up to the task.

Caregiving tested my skills and my mettle.

"I won't put you in a nursing home," I promised John. He sighed with relief.

When I made the promise, I knew without a doubt that John would do the same for me. He would be a kind, loving, and tender caregiver. John was in a wheelchair, but we were together. He could still have "quality of life." But what did "quality of life" mean?

Quality of Life

Health care professionals often use these words. A *Forbes* article, "Quality of Life: Everyone Wants It, But What is It?" defined the term. According to the article, quality of life referred to the positive and negative features of life.[14] For John, quality of life meant having a satisfying life, one that made him happy. I couldn't guarantee John's happiness, but I could foster it.

Many factors contribute to quality of life: physical health, emotional health, family customs, education, financial status, religious or spiritual beliefs, perception, and available support services. I believed I could sustain John's existing quality of life. Though life wasn't what it used to be, John could still have happy experiences. He enjoyed being with his family most of all.

Arranging for John's quality of life was a tiring, complex, never-ending task that sapped my energy. Basically, I had two extra jobs: caregiver and quality arranger. These jobs were in addition to running our household, managing our finances, and planning social events. I used existing skills and developed new ones. This was intense "on-the-job" training, and I learned quickly. But there weren't enough hours in a day. Getting John up, helping him shower, and dressing him were a physical challenge. I felt I'd done a day's work before the day began. Caregiving included other tasks as well:

Schedule John's medical appointments.

Drive John to appointments and stay with him.

Renew prescriptions as needed.

Fix our meals.

Manage finances and pay bills.

Get the car serviced when needed.

Do daily laundry.

---

14 IESE Business School, "Quality of Life: Everyone Wants It, But What is It?" *Forbes*, September 4, 2013, https://www.forbes.com/sites/iese/2013/09/04/quality-of-life-everyone-wants-it-but-what-is-it/?sh=3715ce52635d.

Plan activities for John.

Pay attention to John's mood changes and feelings.

Health Care Challenges

Health care skills were a separate category of care. I was familiar with sterile technique, and washed my hands and wore protective gloves. However, I hadn't practiced hospital sterile technique. I didn't know how to care for a stoma—an opening in the stomach connected to the urinary system. I didn't know anything about catheterization, but I learned. I felt like I was earning a nursing degree the hard way and on my own. No classes. No exams. Just daily, dawn-to-dusk work.

Medication management was a job by itself. I allowed lots of lead time when I ordered John's medications to make sure they arrived on time.

Most of John's medications were mailed to him. Other medications—the ones he needed immediately—came from a local pharmacy. The pharmacy delivered prescriptions to Charter House. With each passing day, John relied on me more and often thanked me.

"I appreciate all you do, and thank you," John said.

"You don't have to thank me, honey," I commented. "I'm your wife, and I love you."

"I want to thank you," he replied gently. His thanks were an expression of love.

I wanted to be a good caregiver, even an excellent caregiver, and I worked so hard to reach this goal that I was tired all the time. To catch up on sleep, I took occasional naps after lunch. When I was going to nap, I told John that I'd sleep for an hour. One hour of sleep could give me the energy I needed until bedtime.

I left the bedroom door ajar so John could find me. When he

wondered where I was, he rolled his wheelchair down the hall, pushed the door open, and peeked at me. Half asleep, I heard him do this. John always wanted me to be close by.

Surprises

Of course, I shopped for groceries, filled the car with gas, and ran errands. Leaving John alone made me anxious, and I was always in a hurry. One time, just as I was about to leave for a hair appointment, John was feeling achy and asked to get back in bed. I helped him transfer, pulled the rolling table next to his bed, handed him a cell phone, and moved his wheelchair within reach. After my haircut, I planned to walk around the mall for exercise but changed my mind.

Something didn't feel right. I went home and found John watching television in the family room. "Did you get out of bed yourself?" I asked.

"No, the firemen helped me," John replied, and went back to watching the program.

Firemen? I was stunned. Did I hear him correctly? Maybe I missed a linking sentence, or my hearing aid needed a new battery.

"What firemen?" I asked worriedly. John's story answered my question.

Shortly after I'd left, a smoke alarm went off. The signal went to our alarm system and a representative called. The man asked John if there was a fire.

"I don't smell any smoke," John answered. "I'm in bed and I'm paraplegic."

Paraplegic was a "go" word, and the representative called the fire department immediately.

Within minutes, a truck had pulled up in front of our townhome and three firemen got out. A fireman called John's cell phone and requested the garage door code. John gave it to him.

The firemen entered the townhome, heard the blaring alarm, and found John in bed. They wanted to conduct a safety check, and John agreed.

"It will be easier and faster if you help me get in my wheelchair," he explained.

The firemen transferred John to his wheelchair. They couldn't stop the fire alarm from blaring, so they finally removed it from the ceiling. The alarm turned out to be defective, and we had a new one installed. This was a scary experience at the time, but it is a humorous memory now, part of family lore. Every time I think of John saying, "The firemen helped me," I smile.

Station Four of the fire department was familiar with our address. John fell, and I called the 911 non-emergency number. The crew arrived quickly with an electronic lifting machine. Getting John up off the floor was a slick maneuver. An electronic cushion was placed under John. This cushion was inflated electronically. When John was at wheelchair height, the firemen slid him into his wheelchair. I was surprised by the equipment and John's story.

At the end of the procedure, a fireman looked around and said, "This place is immaculate. You should see some of the places we visit."

Nobody had ever commented on my cleaning skills, so I appreciated the fireman's comment. Doing laundry every day helped our place look neat and tidy.

Laundry was a top priority, and I often did it at night. John always stashed tissues in his pants pocket. I would check the pockets for tissues before I washed his pants. Sometimes I forgot to check the pockets and the tissues went through the wash and dry cycles.

"It's happened again," John announced as he removed a clump of dried tissues from his pocket. The shrunken, stiff tissues resembled a hockey puck.

"I'm so sorry," I sighed.

"It's okay," John soothed. "I know you're tired."

"Well, it's hard to get good help these days!" I exclaimed. John knew I referred to myself and grinned.

Laundry duty turned into a one-act play. One evening I was so tired I was punchy. When I finished doing laundry, I folded the clothes and put them in the laundry basket. The basket was so full I could hardly see where I was going. I entered our apartment, turned left, and fell into the open dishwasher. Leaving the door open was a sign of my fatigue.

Our coffee pot was on the counter above the dishwasher. John was just about to pour himself some coffee when I fell. He couldn't believe his eyes.

"What's happening?" he asked.

"I fell into the dishwasher," I answered.

"Jeez, are you hurt?" John asked.

"No, the laundry basket and clothes cushioned my fall," I assured him. "I'm okay."

I picked up the scattered clothes, folded them again, and inspected the dishwasher. There was a small dent in the inside rim, an annoying flaw, but not one that would cause the dishwasher to leak. John watched all this from his wheelchair and continued to look shocked.

"Hey, not everyone can fall into a dishwasher," I joked. "It takes special circumstances and talent." The dishwasher incident made it crystal clear that we needed outside help.

Outside Help

Finding help would be easy. All I had to do was look up caregiving agencies online. After I read dozens of posts and developed eye strain, I found two local agencies that matched John's needs.

Their policies differed significantly. One agency had a four-hour minimum a day; the other had a three-hour minimum. We only needed an hour and a half of care, two hours at the most. Maybe I could work something out.

There were two kinds of care available: companion care and personal care. Companion care included things like playing cards, looking at photos, baking cookies, and going for walks with the patient. Personal care included helping with bathing, dressing, and lifting the patient if necessary.

Caregivers with the most training received the most pay. John needed personal care. The minimum hourly rate for personal caregivers was about $23 per hour. After talking with several caregivers about their pay, I learned they didn't receive very much. The agency's fee had to cover operating costs, maintenance, cost of utilities, staff wages, and insurance—overhead that diluted caregivers' wages.

Because I always monitored the budget, I chose the agency with the fewest minimum hours and lowest hourly rate. John agreed with my choice. We looked forward to having outside help. In the beginning, the same caregiver came almost every day, and we loved her.

Sue was cheerful, funny, and efficient. She took care of John for months. Having the same caregiver gave John continuity of care—something he needed and appreciated. Unfortunately for us, the caregiver took a second job and came less frequently. We missed her. John missed her banter (she really was funny), and I missed her practicality.

Caregivers came and went, passing through like a revolving door. I couldn't keep pace with the spinning. We couldn't depend on our caregivers in the winter. No-shows happened too often. I canceled the first agency and enrolled John in another one. We hoped the second agency would be better than the first.

Training the Caregiver

All the caregivers, except for one, were kind and efficient. The new caregiver asked so many questions that I had to demonstrate the tasks. I showed her where the supplies were stored and how to use the standing frame. I also showed her how to transfer John to his shower wheelchair, help him shower, and get him dressed. This information went in one ear and out the other. The next day, the caregiver asked the same questions, and I repeated the demonstrations.

When she showed up on the third day and asked the same questions, I was annoyed. I tried to get the caregiver to be more helpful and failed.

"I don't know how to do that," she said several times.

What did she know?

John witnessed these conversations and became angry. "You're doing everything, and she isn't doing anything," he declared. "We're paying her to watch you work. That's not right." I didn't feel it was right either.

This experience made me think about training. How much training was required for someone to be a caregiver? In Minnesota, one only needs a high school diploma. That's not much education for such important work. Several caregivers were nursing students. Other caregivers, who were not nursing students, had other valuable skills. I valued their skills because I had less energy and was short of breath.

Heart Surgery

Something was very wrong. I knew scarlet fever had damaged my heart as a child, so I checked with my primary care physician. She referred me to a cardiologist. He said I had three leaking valves, the mitral valve being the worst, and I needed corrective surgery. "I'm a few years younger than you, and I've had heart surgery," the cardiologist told me. I didn't know if he had open-heart or transcatheteral surgery (catheter inserted in the groin), or if he had a pig valve, like me, or a metal valve, but I received the message loud and clear.

If he'd survived heart surgery, I would survive it too.

I listened to his diagnosis calmly and wondered if my health care team had made a mistake. Did the medical records get mixed up? Were they really talking about me?

The cardiologist referred me to the lead surgeon, and he advised surgery as soon as possible. We set a date for surgery, and I checked off the days on the calendar. The day for surgery finally came, and I was so panicked I shared my feelings with John.

"I may not survive this," I said worriedly. "I'm scared to the marrow of my bones."

"You'll be fine," he assured me. Open-heart surgery was a major surgery, and I wasn't as confident of the outcome.

My grandson drove me to the hospital. I took the elevator to the cardiac floor, checked in, and waited. An aide approached me, said a patient had canceled and that my surgery was next. I donned a hospital gown and was transferred to a gurney. The anesthesiologist greeted me and checked my name and clinic number. I answered, but before I said another word, I was out.

My mitral valve was replaced with a pig valve. The valve wasn't the pig's actual valve; it was a valve made from living parts. The cardiologist told me it took an entire day to make one valve. Just as John predicted, I survived surgery, spent five days in rehab, and was dismissed. What a happy surprise! Now I could get back to caring for John.

After surgery I felt like a new person, renewed in body and spirit.

Burnout and Compassion Fatigue

John's illnes progressed and self-care became harder. I felt like I was playing a bad game of catch-up. No matter how hard I tried, I never caught up with caregiving tasks, and there were always unchecked items on my to-do list. I wondered if I'd make it through the day. When I was alone and honest with myself, I worried about burnout.

Burnout can take years to develop. The caregiver's feelings progress from enthusiasm (when they are first hired), to stagnation (too much work, too little time), to frustration (not being able to do the work), and finally, apathy (the result of exhaustion). Even trained, dedicated health care workers are subject to burnout. I could be at risk of burnout or compassion fatigue.

Compassion fatigue is a form of burnout—physical, emotional, and spiritual exhaustion. Unlike burnout, which develops slowly, compassion fatigue comes on quickly. It happens when someone cares too much. I thought about John all the time and hoped I wouldn't have compassion fatigue. The holidays put additional pressure on me.

I wanted to stop compassion fatigue before it stopped me.

Controlling and Focusing Thoughts

I did this by controlling my thoughts. The idea came from Dr. Amit Sood, author of *The Mayo Clinic Guide to Stress-Free Living*. "As soon as you wake up, before you get out of bed, let your first thoughts be one of gratitude," Dr. Sood advises.[15]

The minute my eyes opened in the morning, I thought of someone who helped me. Other names came to mind. Each day, I thought of five people. Five more people the next day, and the

---

15 Amit Sood, *The Mayo Clinic Guide to Stress-Free Living* (New York: Hachette Books, 2013), 66.

next. I had a list of people who were kind, smart, and had my back. The mental exercise caused me to remember people from my past, and I was humbled by their kindness. Dr. Sood believes that having a theme for each day of the week helps to reduce stress:

Monday: gratitude
Tuesday: compassion
Wednesday: acceptance
Thursday: higher meaning
Friday: forgiveness
Saturday: celebration
Sunday: reflection and prayer[16]

This sounded like a beneficial approach. I followed his advice but did it differently. Since I couldn't remember all the themes, I chose one I could easily remember: love.

This theme meshed with every day of caregiving. Thinking about love reduced my stress and helped me get through the day. Love reminded me of why I was John's caregiver. His love helped me find my way through the caregiving maze. The maze had twists, turns, and corners. I would deal with an issue, turn a corner, and another challenge appeared. But there was always love at the end of the day.

Financial Worries

The caregiving maze was large and complex. Legal considerations and health care insurance were part of the maze. John's health care insurance covered most of his costs.

Medicare paid for John's hospital bed (the basic model). Within a few months, the mattress sagged in the middle and made John uncomfortable. He slept on the mattress until he learned there

---

16 Sood, *Guide to Stress-Free Living*, 92–95.

was a level-two mattress available. Considering John's health, I didn't understand why he didn't get the better mattress first.

In the long run, I think this decision would have saved Medicare some money. At the time, caregiving agencies didn't supply employees with exam gloves, so we paid for them. We spent $850 a year on gloves alone. I've always been cautious about spending money, and the mounting costs of health care made me more cautious. I watched every penny we spent.

Going into debt wasn't going to happen on my watch. I became more cautious about personal spending. Dozens of mail-order catalogs were delivered to our post office box. Page by page, I looked through them and found a few articles of clothing I liked, but I didn't order them. I knew the difference between want and need, but one ad captivated me.

"I might order a sweater," I told John worriedly.

"Go ahead and order it," he assured me. "I like to see you in nice clothes."

I ordered the sweater and loved it, and so did John.

"We have enough money to buy you decent clothes," he assured me. "Buy what you need."

After this exchange, I bought new clothes but not many. Having too many clothes in the closet made me nervous.

John's Physical Therapy

John's strength was failing, so I hired a physical therapist. She helped him do exercises to strengthen his legs. For a while, John's legs were stronger, and then his progress stalled. He couldn't do some of the exercises and became upset. He didn't get upset in front of his physical therapist, but he revealed his feelings to me. "My legs aren't working," he declared. John had such a worried expression on his face, I gasped.

"That may be temporary," I replied. I didn't say anything else because I didn't know what to say.

After twenty-three years of caregiving, after everything I'd accomplished, guilt reared its ugly head. Guilt was a debilitating emotion, and few good things—if any—came from it. I knew this, yet I couldn't get rid of my feelings and they just kept coming. Damn guilt.

I felt guilty about my limited nursing skills.

I felt guilty when I ordered new clothes.

I felt guilty if I went for a haircut.

I felt guilty when I was impatient with John.

I felt guilty for some things I said.

I felt guilty for feeling guilty.

What a mishmash of feelings. I talked with other caregivers, and they all said they felt guilty. Apparently, guilt is a common feeling among caregivers. The reasons for these feelings can be small, silly, or significant such as a family feud. Reading about guilt was helpful, but it didn't make it go away. In his final days, about two weeks before John died, I felt guilty about enrolling John in hospice care. However, I did this at the suggestion of the nurse practitioner in charge of the supportive care unit.

Palliative vs. Hospice Care

Palliative care is specialized care for patients with serious illnesses, but the patient is expected to live for some time. This type of care can help improve a patient's quality of life, such as medication management, necessary changes in diet, and religious or spiritual support. A patient in palliative care can still receive chemotherapy, radiation, and dialysis.

Hospice care is end-of-life care for patients; the patient won't be cured. John's end-of-life care included medication management, changes in diet (he hardly ate anything), pain management, and emotional support.

"Medicare will pay for hospice care," the nurse practitioner assured me.

I arranged for hospice care with a local agency.

"Why did you sign me up?" John asked.

"Well, I think the unit may be short-staffed right now," I answered. "It's always helpful to have another set of eyes." This placated John, but he didn't believe it. He was a physician and knew the end was near.

The agency asked about the kind of care I needed for John.

"Straightening the room would be helpful," I replied. "John might also want to talk with someone about his experiences in Vietnam."

After a hospice person visited John, I could tell they had been there. The pile of newspapers was gone. Pillows were neatly piled on the unoccupied second bed. The room looked better, and John felt better. A staff member talked with John about his wartime experiences.

"I think he wanted to do it," she shared.

I became John's advocate. When I had to explain myself, I did well. This situation was different; advocacy was a new role for me. Many hospitals have advocacy departments to support patients and their families. If a patient felt they were treated unfairly, or if family members were confused, nurses, social workers, chaplains, and other staff members were there to help.

But I wasn't a nurse, social worker, or chaplain. I was a one-woman advocacy department and out of my comfort zone. I gradually eased into the advocacy role. One experience was especially painful. After John had a second operation to repair his aorta, he was transferred to a nursing home to recover.

Days after he was admitted to the nursing home, the social worker visited him and decided he needed psychological counseling. I tracked down the social worker and asked why she had made this decision.

"John cried," she explained. "I visited him twice and he cried twice."

The social worker didn't seem to know much about John's medical history. Without telling me or John, she ordered counseling. Counseling after a traumatic experience was something I understood, but I thought John's case was different.

The Advocate Role

After John's second surgery for a dissected aorta in 2013, he had been in the Intensive Care Unit (ICU) for weeks and in a medication-induced coma. Nurses gradually awakened John from the coma, a process that took several days. When he woke up, John's arms and legs didn't work. The feeling in his arms returned, but the feeling in his legs did not. In addition, John was sleep-deprived, didn't eat normal meals, or remember family visits.

I'd cry too if I had experienced all this. John needed time— time to think about his surgery, his stay in intensive care, his long recuperation, and living life in a wheelchair. He deserved this time. I put on my advocacy hat, mustered my courage, and took a deep breath.

"John doesn't need counseling," I said to the social worker. "He is recovering from ICU psychosis."

I could tell by her expression that she had never heard of the disorder. ICU psychosis is a term used to describe the confusion, delirium, and disorientation caused by being in intensive care. According to the article, "Medical Definition of ICU Psychosis," one patient in three who spends more than five days in the ICU has this reaction.

"Something about the ICU causes some people who are already experiencing great debility, stress, and pain to 'lose their minds.' "[17]

I didn't lose my mind. I spoke my mind and told John's story quickly.

"John had life-threatening surgery—four physicians, thirteen hours. He was in the ICU for weeks. He was in a coma, hooked up to beeping machines, and on strong pain meds. When nurses brought him out of the coma, his legs didn't work. John didn't get much sleep, didn't eat regular meals, didn't remember family visits. He still has drugs in his system."

Then I delivered the punch line. "I refuse to pay for counseling."

While the social worker had good intentions (she wouldn't have become a social worker if she didn't), ordering counseling without telling me or John was a mistake. John was vulnerable, and her decision hurt him. Now it was up to me to fix things. The social worker gave me a phone number and told me to call the number to stop counseling. Wasn't that her job?

The person I spoke with was sympathetic and only charged me $50 instead of billing me the full amount. This experience made me realize the need for patient advocacy, a topic John and I discussed many times.

"What happens to patients who don't have an advocate?" he asked. "What happens if they don't have a Harriet?"

My advocacy role continued for years. I represented John again when he was transferred to nursing care at Charter House. Because of COVID-19, the unit didn't allow any visitors on the floor. John became depressed when he wasn't able to see me. I

17 Jay W. Marks, "Medical Definition of ICU Psychosis," MedicineNet, June 3, 2021, https://www.medicinenet.com/icu_psychosis/definition.htm.

sent an email to the director and nursing supervisor explaining the situation and asking for permission to visit John.

"I've been John's advocate for sixty-three years," I wrote, "and will continue to be his advocate." My request was approved. This experience, and many others, made me realize I had to become my own advocate. I had to do a better job of self-care.

Self-Care through Art

I searched the Internet for information about Japanese ensō circles. This art form, a version of Japanese brush painting, comes from Buddhism. An ensō circle represents the circle of life, strength, and knowledge. I bought a large pad of paper, an ink brush, and a jar of black ink.

Before I painted an ensō, I meditated for several minutes. Then I dipped my brush into the ink and painted a circle with one stroke. Historically, ensō circles were supposed to be painted with one stroke, two at the most. Today, artists create ensō circles with watercolors and metallic paint, and add decorations and inspirational words. I painted Japanese circles for weeks and switched to doodle art—a combination of ordinary doodling, comics, and folk art. This was a change that happened accidentally.

While quarantined because of COVID-19, I wrote two grief workbooks for kids: one for ages nine to twelve, and another for ages four to eight. The publisher sent me copies of the illustrations, and they were charming. This was the first doodle art I noticed. Why hadn't I heard about doodle art before? Then the answer came to me. Because I cared for three generations of family members, I missed the beginning of the trend.

Since I had an MA in art education, I thought I could create doodle art. Learning the techniques was easy. Doodle art became my morning wake-up activity. I doodled for fifteen minutes every morning. I felt refreshed and ready to return to caregiving after finishing a doodle. This went on for months. I explained doodle art to John, but he didn't get it.

"I don't know a doodle from a noodle," he admitted.

When he saw my art, however, John understood it and encouraged me. I continued to be grateful for his encouragement.

Planning a Nothing Day

"Today I'm going to have a Nothing Day," I said. "I'm going to sit on the couch, put my feet up, read if I want to, take a nap, or stare straight ahead."

John understood because he had seen me care for three generations of family members.

"Don't worry," I assured him. "You'll still get your medications and meals."

John trusted me, knew I'd take care of him, and approved of the idea. Each month, I tried to have a Nothing Day, and developed a repertoire of activities. I logged in to caregiving websites. I wrote affirmations, so many they became a book. Baking was recreation for me, and I made cookies from scratch. Since writing is in my bones, I brainstormed ideas for future articles and books.

I wrote an article about Nothing Days, which Mayo Clinic included in its online publication, *Experts by Experience*. Nothing Days benefited me and John. The most important part of self-care, however, was being with John. We were together.

Self-care evolved into positive self-talk. I told myself I was doing my best. This changed to, "I'm doing my best with the time I have." This changed to, "I'm doing my best with the time I have and the skills I've learned." When I looked back on my twenty-three years of caregiving, I could say, with all honesty, I did my best.

Older adults often neglect dental care. Not me. Dental health is related to heart disease—a surprising fact. I wanted to care for my heart and my teeth. Since I'd been going to the same dentist for years, I continued to see him. I went for dental check-ups and cleaning every six months. Having my teeth cleaned wasn't one of my favorite activities, but it was necessary. I take a prescribed antibiotic before going to the dentist.

Though my socialization times were limited, I made time for those who mattered. John wanted me to socialize with others. I met friends for coffee and volunteered for a few committees. I continued to attend meetings of the Study Club—something I'd been doing for years. Each member of the Study Club served as a hostess once or twice and wrote a research paper. Most of my papers were about art or writing, and I once wrote about Robert Frost. The Study Club was more than learning—it was a source of group support, and I tapped that source several times.

These breaks made me a better caregiver for John and recharged me. The benefits of caregiving also recharged me: sharing memories, making new memories, continuity of care, being together, and planning a future for me. The benefits endured after John died, and each one was a stepping stone to the future.

Caregiving tasks proved I could still learn. I didn't have memory disease—thank goodness—or a faulty mind, or huge obstacles to overcome. Yes, it took longer than I thought to polish some skills, but I learned them. I was proud of myself. Learning continues to be an important part of my life. Without learning, I wouldn't be me.

Caregiving is Love

I created a new daily routine, and we depended on it. The day was different if the caregiver was a no-show. John was willing to skip his shower, which helped me greatly. Getting John ready for the day was a day's work. If I got John up by myself, I was tired for the rest of the day.

Caregiving reminded me of the miracle of life. The fact that we were together was a miracle. We watched television together in the evenings, John in his wheelchair and me in the rocking chair next to him. Choosing what programs to watch was a joint decision. John liked having me by his side, and sometimes we held hands.

During the seven years I cared for John, we became more devoted to each other. Love didn't have to be expressed with words. Being in the same room with John was a loving experience. Eating together was a loving experience. Reading together was a loving experience. Kissing John goodnight was one of the best loving experiences. Love was a simple theme for the day, and I lived it each day.

Caregiving was love in action.

I was asked to write a few words for a caregiving meeting at church. This was easy because I'd written four books and dozens of articles about caregiving. The challenge was to distill my thoughts in a few words. After several false starts, I found my niche and wrote these words:

Some days, when we are burdened, the hours are dark.

Some days, when we are tired, we think we can't go on.

Some days, when we are afraid, we forget about courage.

Some days, when we are sad, we do not hear an inner voice.

Thankfully, these days are balanced by others.

Each day, family members brighten our lives.

Each day, church friends are ready to help.

Each day, we discover courage again.

Each day, there is an inner flame within us.

A flame that leads to a joyful life.

Chapter 7

Renewal Is an Inside Job

"Grief strikes the brain the moment news of a death reaches it," writes brain expert Dorothy Holinger.[18] This sentence seemed to be written for me.

Holinger described my reaction to death in one sentence, and grief struck my brain many times. My experience with death began in fifth grade when our cocker spaniel, Timmy, was hit by a car and died. I watched my father bury our dog by the apple tree in the backyard. I didn't want to watch, but I couldn't turn away. I cried and cried.

In later years, friends and colleagues referred to me as an "experienced griever." I believed the deaths of family members would hurt less over time. My assumption was wrong. Every death was an assault on my brain and my body.

Though shock became a familiar feeling, it was strong and harmful. When John died, a part of me died too. His death affected many areas of my life: marriage, security, support, knowledge, and self-expression.

I knew John for sixty-seven years. He was devoted to me, and I was devoted to him. Our respect for each other was evident to everyone. He was a thoughtful husband and enjoyed surprising me. One Christmas he walked in through the door carrying one of the largest poinsettia plants I'd ever seen.

18 Dorothy P. Holinger, *The Anatomy of Grief: How the Brain, Heart, and Body Can Heal after Loss* (New Haven, CT: Yale University Press, 2020), 75.

"What a surprise!" I exclaimed. "That isn't a plant, it's a tree."

My Amazing Husband

John was my protector. He came to my rescue if I was threatened or hurt. We went to Egypt in our fifties, and two scary-looking men approached me. I was standing alone while John was talking to a friend a few feet away. John turned to check on me, saw the men, rushed to my side, and shouted, "Get away from my wife!" The men realized I wasn't alone and left abruptly.

John was my cheerleader. He wanted me to decorate the house however I wanted, pursue my hobbies, have new interests, and continue my writing career. Before I started a new book, I shared my ideas with him. We discussed the purpose, the cover, and target markets. If John had any thoughts, he shared them gently. "Are you sure you want to do that?" After a book was released, John was as excited as I was; my joy was his joy. He told others about my published books and current writing projects.

John was my medical adviser. I would ask John if I had a medical question or about worrisome symptoms. Was the symptom serious? Did I need to go to the emergency department? Our dinner-time conversations were often medical conversations. We talked about the spread of COVID-19, its symptoms, and its variants.

John was my confidant. Everyone needs a confidant, someone they can trust, and John was mine. We laughed every day and cared for one another. Unlike some men, John shared his feelings easily, and I treasured these sharing times. Each of us usually knew what the other was thinking. Most of the time we had the same feelings.

John was my husband and I loved him fiercely. The absence of a protector, cheerleader, medical adviser, confidant, and husband were blows to my identity. I wanted to be whole again. To do this, I had to accept life and death. Acceptance wouldn't happen without a willingness to change. It could be a far-off goal I would never reach, so I shook the puzzle pieces of my life out of an imaginary box, studied them, and fit them together as best I could.

Putting myself together without John's help was tough, but I did it. I tried to be proactive—a tall order for anyone, especially for someone who is grieving.

"You can do this," I said to myself. "You will do this."

The Comfort of a Poem

Of course, I knew my loved ones were gone forever. Yet the finality of this realization cut right through me. I posted John's photo on the refrigerator along with his favorite poem. Having the poem where I could see it comforted me. Every time I opened the refrigerator, I read the poem. In the morning, I looked at his photo and said, "Hi, honey."

Oh my God, was I losing it? After I read the poem aloud, I thought about it, felt better, and decided I wasn't losing it. I was missing John.

The poem was "Look to This Day," attributed to Kalidasa, one of India's greatest poets. The opening lines stated John's philosophy in simple words: "Look to this day! For it is life, the very life of life."[19]

I wanted to look to each day in memory of John. But posting John's photo and the poem weren't signs of acceptance; they were signs of half acceptance.

About a year later, I stopped greeting John's photo in the morning, a sign of true acceptance. I told stories about him without sobbing. I made legal and financial decisions on my own.

---

19 Kalidasa, "Look to this Day," 4–5th century A.D.

John thought I was money smart, and if he believed in me, I believed in me. My progress was slow, yet I was moving forward with life. I had the wisdom that comes with aging.

Eighty-seven birthdays taught me that endings were really beginnings. With courage, patience, and honesty, I could begin again. I *had* to begin again, and my personality type worked in my favor.

Influence of Personality

Many researchers, including Carl Jung, studied personality types and identified them. But researchers had different ideas about the number of personality types. A recent study divided personalities into four basic types: average, reserved, role models, and self-centered.[20] My personality fit somewhere between average and role model. Thankfully, at age eight-seven, I knew and understood my personality pretty well.

I wasn't the kind of person who sat around. I needed to be busy and wanted to be busy. The happy, loving relationship I had with John worked in my favor. Some people I knew were so angry at their loved ones for dying they could barely see straight. Not me. I was an upbeat person and used this trait to my advantage. In the midst of grief, I found positives in my life and was grateful for them.

I focused on the present. But some of the phone calls I received almost shattered me. John's first name was Corrin, a name that came from his Manx heritage. For legal and professional purposes, he went by C. John. Grief grabbed me by the throat when I received phone calls that began with, "Is Corrin there?" I was barely able to speak.

---

20 Meghan Holohan, "Study Finds 4 Main Personality Types—Which One Are You?" *Today*, September 20, 2018, https://www.today.com/health/personality-types-average-self-centered-role-model-or-reserved-t137902.

"He's not available now," I replied. "May I take a message?" I used this answer every time I received a call asking for Corrin. Nobody wanted to leave a message.

Despite notifying many organizations of John's death, I continued to receive mail addressed to him. Looking at these letters was painful. Even more painful, I had to contact the organizations again and ask for John's name to be removed from their mailing lists. I contacted some organizations several times, which added to the pain I felt.

Heart Problems

The pig valve in my heart was supposed to correct a heart defect and improve function, but I started having bouts of atrial fibrillation, which scared me. These spells increased after John died. Many people can't feel their changes in heart rhythm, but I can, and it felt like something heavy was pushing on my chest. I checked my blood pressure and measured my oxygen level with an oximeter. The oximeter showed I was having atrial fibrillation. I called 911 and went to the emergency department three times in ten days. I felt like I was keeping the Mayo Clinic Ambulance Service in business.

Despite the excellent care I received, going to the emergency department was upsetting. I missed John's gentle words of assurance. I cried the first time I went to the emergency department by myself. A member of the health care team offered to tell me about the schedule, what would happen first, what would happen second, and follow-up procedures.

"Don't bother," I replied. "I've been in the emergency department so often I could work here."

Maybe grief had something to do with my atrial fibrillation. According to Holinger, grief affects the survivor's health. "Any number of a widower's or a widow's functions and organs may become compromised, not least the heart itself."[21] Wow, this was upsetting news.

My doctor ordered a variety of tests and changed one of my medications. The change helped, but it didn't solve my atrial fibrillation problems. I started taking a medication that controls heart rhythm after several cardiologists recommended it. The medicine worked but had many side effects, and I wasn't supposed to take it for very long.

Despite the scary side effects, the medication helped, and I had A-Fib less often. Still, the cardiologist worried about the side effects of the medication and took me off it because it didn't help me that much. My heart problems were a reality check, and I faced other realities alone.

I had a limited number of years left. Was I running out of time? Would I have enough time to do what I wanted to do?

Still Setting Goals

Elizabeth Harper Neeld measures time differently. Neeld divides time into two groups—*chronos* and *kairos*—two words I hadn't encountered before.

Chronos time is chronological time measured on a calendar.

Kairos time is inner time, "moments of awakening," and living mindfully.[22]

I needed to accept the things I couldn't change. Acceptance was pain upon pain. My elder daughter's story would always be unfinished. I could have been a better caregiver and wished I had done some things differently. The relationship with my brother

---

21 Holinger, *Anatomy of Grief*, 229.

22 Elizabeth Harper Neeld, "How Long Is This Grieving Going to Last?" Legacy, January 3, 2017, https://www.legacy.com/news/how-long-is-this-grieving-going-to-last/.

would never be resolved. I wished I'd said "I love you" more often. I wished I could take back some of the words I said.

What had I accomplished? I graduated from college, earned a graduate degree, taught for a dozen years, raised two daughters, was a "mom" for Golden Retrievers, raised twin grandchildren, wrote forty-four books, gave workshops on various topics, volunteered in the community, and had a variety of interests. All in all, a decent list of accomplishments.

What did I hope to yet accomplish? I wanted to write another book, see great-grandchildren more often, learn new skills, and make new friends. Making new friends wasn't easy. Caring for John limited my Charter House contacts, and I hardly knew anyone. Residents had to wear masks, so I hardly recognized anyone and couldn't understand what they said.

Making new friends was difficult because hundreds of people live at Charter House and I don't know all their names. Some residents asked if I had just moved in because they didn't recognize me or know my name. I formed interpersonal relationships with several staff members. They recognized me even though I wore a mask, and said, "Hello, Mrs. Hodgson." Their kindness touched my heart.

Being in a Documentary

I was surprised when Charter House informed us that award-winning French filmmakers, Sylvie Gilman and Thierry de Lestrade, were at Mayo Clinic to shoot footage for a documentary about aging. Mayo Clinic was the next to last stop on their fact-finding trip. Thierry was the director and photographer, and Sylvie was the translator and writer.

The filmmakers asked to interview two Charter House residents, one male and female. I was chosen to be interviewed. Being in a documentary film wasn't one of my goals, but it was a total surprise and serendipitous experience. The interview was supposed to take place in a rental apartment, but the filmmakers wanted something more home-like and came to my apartment instead. Thank goodness my apartment was neat and tidy and the filmmakers liked the setting.

They filmed me standing next to John's antique clock, which ticked loudly.

"The clock says good life, good life, good life," I commented. The filmmakers seemed to like that line.

"You're going to be a star in France," Sylvie enthused. I knew that would never happen but smiled anyway.

Thierry filmed me in John's former bedroom, which had been cleared of medical equipment. There was a montage of photos on the wall of my father-in-law, brother-in-law, and John. Sylvie asked me about the photos. I identified family members and stated their occupations—Dad, a specialist in diseases of the chest; my brother-in-law, a specialist in endocrinology; and John, a specialist in aerospace, aviation, and internal medicine.

"John was my champion and defender," I declared. "I have a new defender, and it's me. You can't wait to be rescued."

Sylvie and Thierry filmed me riding an exercise bike in the wellness center. Filming was supposed to continue outdoors, but a sudden downpour of rain changed our plans. According to the forecast, the storm would be gone in about an hour.

"We'll wait in the lobby downstairs," Sylvie said. "We'll continue filming when the weather clears. You have time to get something to eat. And remember to wear the same clothes."

I had a quick dinner, and as luck would have it, dripped food on my shirt. *Oh no!* I spot-cleaned the shirt and dried it with a hair dryer. Just as I was about to leave the apartment, my daughter called.

"I can't talk to you now," I explained. "A French film crew is here, and we're about to film the next scene in the park across the street."

My daughter thought that was hilarious, and she still thinks it's hilarious.

"Why was that funny?" I asked later.

"It was outlandish," she countered. "What was happening to my mom? It was so real and unreal. I guess you never know when a French film crew will knock on your door."

The filmmakers asked me to sit on a park bench and "look pensive." I wasn't sure how to do that, so I winged it. After they left, I sent a thank-you email to Sylvie and Thierry. Because resilience was front and center in my mind, I suggested a documentary about the topic.

"If we ever make a film about resilience," Sylvie replied, "you will be in it."

Being in a documentary was unexpected, to say the least, and it yanked me out of my comfort zone. The experience renewed me and made me focus on the future. I wouldn't be interviewed for more documentaries, but I could do exciting and unexpected things. If my time was limited, I decided to finish with a flourish, a crescendo at the end of my life symphony.

Setbacks

Still, I never knew when setbacks, such as anniversary reactions, would knock on my door. Anniversary reactions can be almost anything—the day your loved one proposed, moving to a new town, or the birth of a child.

Crying on the anniversary of John's birthday was a setback. I thought about past birthdays and all the cakes I'd baked for him. John's favorite birthday meal was marinated flank steak, which is also one of my favorite meals.

Finding a baby photo of Helen was a setback. The photo

was tucked in a drawer. In the photo, my toddler daughter was wearing corduroy overalls and licking frosting from a beater. She looked pleased.

Setting my mother's glass water bottle on the Thanksgiving table was a setback. The bottle came from England and symbolized her heritage. Though the bottle reminded me of my mother's death, it was a linking object to her life.

Like all who grieve, I experienced many setbacks, and they worried me. Was I going backward in life, backward on my healing path, and stuck in the past?

My worry about setbacks resulted in a major decision. I could let grief destroy me or grow from it. I decided to grow from grief, and from that moment on, thought of myself as a winning person.

Crying bouts weren't steps backward; they were steps forward—tests to see if I was ready for the future.

Jeffrey A. Kottler, author of *The Language of Tears*, says crying represents the worst and best of being alive.[23] I looked at crying bouts as opportunities to examine and release feelings. Like other communication tools—articles, discussion, debate, social media, and email—tears could be bridges to friendship. I was willing to cross those bridges.

New Thoughts and Directions

Grief reminded me of the preciousness of each day, hour, and moment. I visualized myself as a winning survivor, determined to feel better, open to possibilities, and open to life. Renewal was something I deserved, and I was determined to make it happen. I gave myself permission to live.

My loved ones would want me to enjoy life. I chose the path of growth and set new goals. I planned for setbacks. Friends told

---

23 Jeffrey A. Kottler, *The Language of Tears* (New York: Wiley, 1996), 215.

me time healed all wounds. Time helped, but in the long run, I healed myself. The process wasn't quick, but it was constant, and that was encouraging.

The focus of my writing changed. I spoke about grief to church groups, community groups, at conferences, and during chapter meetings of the Compassionate Friends. I gave workshops about grief doodling. These changes came about because I lived in kairos time. To do this, I needed to go inward and make time for reflection. No denial. No half-truths. No lies.

Reflection helped me in the past, but it was different this time.

Too many pictures were stored in my mind, many of them happy and many of them sad. The image of John in the ICU, in a coma and hooked up to life-support machines, was seared in my mind. Even though it was a painful image to remember, surgeons saved John's life, and he lived seven more years. The picture reminded me of the excellent care John received.

Family members and friends said I was resilient. I wasn't sure what resilience looked like. To these people, apparently resilience looked like me. I checked the online dictionary for synonyms of resilience and the last one, "reawaken," caught my attention. It symbolized my new mission in life.

Finding New Meaning

David Kessler, author of *Finding Meaning*, thinks this process is the sixth stage of grief, and helps us find a way forward. Searching for new meaning was an empowering idea. Meaning is relative for each person. "When one finds meaning, it doesn't feel like the death of a loved one [or loved ones] was worth it . . . Meaning is what *you* make happen," Kessler explains.[24]

---

24 David Kessler, *Finding Meaning: The Sixth Stage of Grief* (New York: Scribner, 2019), 71–72.

I could only find meaning by myself and for myself. Unhealthy grieving wasn't for me. I remembered the vow I made after my daughter died: *Death will be the loser. Life will be the winner. I will make it so.*

Kessler compares the original meaning of events with new meanings. After I read his comparisons, I came up with my own.

Old meaning: John died because I didn't do enough.
New meaning: I did all I could.

Old meaning: I don't know why he died now.
New meaning: John had come to the end of his life.

Old meaning: I have so many sad stories.
New meaning: Everyone has sad stories.

Old meaning: There were weaknesses in my caregiving.
New meaning: That's the nature of caregiving.

Old meaning: I haven't been a good friend lately.
New meaning: Friends understood my situation.

Old meaning: I should have stopped writing.
New meaning: Writing helped me figure things out.

Deciding to thrive was the first step in finding meaning. The day after John died, I woke up and my first thoughts were, "I am alive. This day is precious, and I will make the most of it."

Actor Christopher Reeve made the most of his life after a terrible accident. According to newspaper and television accounts at the time, Reeve was riding his horse when it stopped suddenly in front of a hurdle. The helmet Reeve was wearing didn't protect his neck. He was thrown to the ground forcefully, his neck was fractured, and Reeve was paralyzed.

After the accident, Reeve asked himself two questions: "Why me?" and "Why not me?"

Reeve searched for new meaning and created it. He cofounded

the Christopher Reeve Foundation with his wife, Dana. Dedicated to spinal cord injury research, the foundation provides mentoring and caregiving services to newly paralyzed patients, and also conducts clinical trials. Their motto, "Today's Care. Tomorrow's Cure," symbolizes the work of the foundation.

Christopher Reeve is best known for his role in *Superman*. He was a real superman, one who found a new and lasting life purpose.

New meaning became a priority. I wondered if I was strong enough to do it. The quest began with my healing path. My past experiences with grief helped me create this path: stages of grief, finding new purpose, setting goals, and planning a future. Some of the steps I took were random, and I was okay with that. Random steps were refreshing.

A New Relationship with Deceased Loved Ones

I wanted to experience "healthy grieving." These words often appear in grief articles and books. Did healthy grieving mean sobbing like crazy, being confused, or having grief brain? None of those sounded healthy to me. As I walked forward on the healing path, I understood the meaning of these words. Healthy grieving required thinking of my deceased loved ones differently and finding new places for them in my life.

Some grief experts said I had to develop a new relationship with the deceased. This idea puzzled me. I thought my loved ones needed to be alive to have a relationship with them. Not true. Developing a new relationship included breaking through emotional barriers until I reached the truth. Four losses in 2007 were too much to handle. Coming to terms with grief took longer for me because I could only think about one person at a time.

I thought about the nature of each relationship: my relationship with my father, mother, brother, father-in-law, mother-in-law, daughter, son-in-law, and John. For the most part, these relationships were good. My mother-in-law, for example, wrote me a note about how much she appreciated my sense of humor. Thinking about relationships was time-consuming, exhausting, and revealing.

I couldn't move forward on the healing path until I had done this thinking. According to grief expert Therese A. Rando, I had to recall the ups and downs of each relationship, the positives and negatives, the crises and joys, and how these relationships changed through the years. Doing this would allow me to have a new relationship with my departed loved ones.[25]

As I thought about each relationship, images from the past came to mind. My father was the air raid warden for our block during World War II. In my mind, I saw him walking up and down the street, checking to make sure the houses were dark. I remembered how serious he was about his job.

I saw my mother baking sponge cakes—her specialty. She was such a superb baker that friends asked her to bake cakes for them. They delivered the ingredients and Mom baked the cakes. Our small kitchen became a cake factory.

I saw my brother's collection of sailing books lined up on a shelf. He read them all. My brother always looked for a sailing book wherever we went, and he had amassed an extensive collection. The book about tying sailing knots was one of his favorites.

I saw my mother-in-law setting the table for a formal dinner. She was a Victorian grandmother and proud of it. Her table settings, which included a "silence cloth" beneath the tablecloth, were worthy of royalty. I wished I could set a table as well.

---

25 Therese A. Rando, *How to Go On Living When Someone You Love Dies* (New York: Random House, 1991), 251.

I saw my father-in-law flying a small plane. He did this for a few years and stopped.

"Now I know what keeps a plane in the air," he said with a chuckle. "Money."

For Dad, that was a joke and wasn't a joke. He quit flying.

I saw Helen sitting at the sewing machine and make a skirt in an hour without reading the instructions. We were astonished. To this day, I can't believe my daughter did this.

I saw my former son-in-law holding his babies. He was proud of them and had a T-shirt that said, "Father of Twins." He was proud to be their dad.

I saw John in his Air Force uniform and colonel's hat. The hat had silver lightning bolts on it, and the jacket was adorned with rows of service ribbons. John represented the Air Force well.

These were happy memories, to be sure. Remembering my loved ones made me think of stories about them. One story was about my mother taking driving lessons.

Since Mom didn't drive, she had to wait until my father could drive her places or, if it wasn't too far, walk to her destination. This became so tiresome, my mother decided to take driving lessons. The first lessons went well, and Mom was pleased with herself until the day she hit the porch with our car.

My brother had a wicked sense of humor. He heard the thump, opened the front door, and shouted, "Did you knock?"

Mom didn't find his comment humorous. In fact, she was so ashamed she gave up on driving lessons. After my father died and Mom moved to Florida, a cousin gave her driving lessons. She passed the test and became a licensed driver, which was a highlight of her life.

I chuckled when I remembered Mom hitting the porch, and then I became teary-eyed.

Tears connected me to the past and were signs of love.

Someone cared about me, and I cared about them. My tears didn't last long, yet they were a relief—proof that life was moving forward. I felt better. I was open to possibilities and planted seeds of renewal.

Stopping Negative Self-Talk

Changing my self-talk was one seed. After a loved one dies, it is natural and normal to have negative thoughts. But I didn't want these thoughts to become a habit. I kept an eye out for the beginning of negative talk, and when I realized it, I put on the brakes. "Harriet, you're heading in the wrong direction. You can stop this negative self-talk." And I did.

When a negative thought came to mind, I balanced it with a positive one. I did this so often it became automatic. Automatic didn't mean less effective. Like driving to reach a destination, thought reversal helped me get to where I wanted to go. I wanted to be a positive, contributing person. And so I began to monitor my chatter, and the conversations I had in my head.

Psychologist Ethan Kross wrote a book on the topic: *Chatter: The Voice in Our Head.* Kross suggests ways to monitor self-talk, starting with distancing yourself from it. To do this, I could refer to myself in the second person.[26] This sounded far-fetched to me, but I tried it and it worked.

Pretending to advise a friend was another way to manage self-talk. This was easy for me. Friends asked me for advice in the past, and I gave it. I didn't have to pretend to give advice; I had done it in real life. If someone felt my advice was beneficial, they heeded it. If they felt my advice wasn't beneficial, they never told me.

---

26 Ethan Kross, *Chatter: The Voice in Our Head, Why It Matters, and How to Harness It* (New York: Penguin Random House, 2021), 72.

Reinterpreting my body's response to stress was another suggestion. The body's response to stress—my body's response to stress—was an adaptive evolutionary reaction, according to Kross.[27] Humans had been doing this for years, and I was aware of my physical responses to the stress of grief, including shortness of breath, dry throat, and bursting into tears without warning. To counter stress I practiced diaphragm breathing, painted ensō circles, and created doodle art.

A third suggestion grabbed my attention: "Normalize your experience."[28] I followed this suggestion by talking with other widows, speaking about my multiple losses, and joining the Compassionate Friends. The Compassionate Friends has a custom that benefits its members. On the second Sunday of December at seven in the evening, bereaved parents, siblings, and grandparents around the world light candles in memory of their deceased loved ones. I participated in this custom and felt a kinship with other bereaved people.

Thousands of bereaved people around the world shared my grief and understood it. This idea empowered me. Strange as it may seem, I felt a sense of belonging. I wasn't alone; I was with my tribe, and despite the odds, the members were strong. Many had created new lives from the ashes of grief.

Helping Others is Renewal

Long ago, I realized that helping others helped me. I encouraged other bereaved people to tell their stories. I became more active in the local Compassionate Friends chapter. I gave workshops on grief healing and reconciliation. I continued to write books

---

27 Kross, *Chatter*, 93.

28 Kross, *Chatter*, 163.

for the bereaved. Writing the books helped me sort my feelings. Positive book reviews empowered me. I was on the right track.

Grief left scars on my life, and I looked for ways to heal them. Instead of a Band-Aid approach, I looked for long-lasting ways to heal my scars, things that added dimension to my life.

No, I wasn't asked to be in another documentary, but I accepted invitations I might have turned down in the past. I spoke to public health departments. I turned a poem I'd written into a children's book, planned the story boards, and paid for the illustrations. I entered books in contests, paid to display them at book fairs, and gave talks that extended my books.

Remember, I came from a generation that was taught not to brag, so these were big steps for me. I was reminded of Dad's sage advice: "Take credit for what you do." I followed his advice with renewed fervor.

Almost every afternoon, I joined the Lobby Ladies, but my comments changed. Rather than being silent about my work, I talked about the chapter I was working on as well as my published and forthcoming books. Though I felt good about doing this, one day I dominated the discussion and felt badly afterward. I apologized to the Lobby Ladies at the next meeting.

"Why are you apologizing?" someone asked. "You've done a lot and can talk about what you've done."

Talking about my books and artwork were signs of renewal. Not recovery. I would never fully recover from multiple losses. Renewal didn't mean I had forgotten my loved ones. The opposite was true: My loved ones continued to be part of my life. I continued to resolve my grief. How did I know I was healing?

My sense of humor returned fully. I laughed often and made others laugh. When I interacted with Charter House residents and staff, I tried to leave a laugh behind. Laughter brightened my days and hopefully theirs as well. I was glad I could still laugh and did it often. Laughter was part of each day.

Happy memories shined brighter than unhappy ones. The decision to leave unhappy memories in the past was a conscious one. When I look back at the years since John died, I can see my progress clearly. Sure, some days all I did was put one step in front of the other, but I made progress. I am proud of this progress and not afraid to say so.

I shared stories of my loved ones.

Some days I forgot about grief.

The confident person I used to be returned.

I planned for anniversary reactions without distress.

New interests were part of my life.

The future looked as bright as the North Star.

I went with the flow.

It took courage to get to this point in my life. Being able to go with the flow was acceptance. I didn't follow a negative flow such as alcoholism, drug addiction, or excessive spending. Instead, I went with a positive flow. I was more open with people, to new experiences, and I benefited from them both.

I connected with relatives, spent time with friends, and laughed more often. One friend said, "You have a marvelous sense of humor," and that made me feel good. Another friend said, "You're so funny you should have been a stand-up comedian." Laughter saved me in the past and continues to save me in the present. I laugh easily, thank goodness. Being able to laugh at myself helped me break out of the grief bubble.

When I broke out of the bubble, I did it with a loud *pop*. No halfway measures for me. I wanted to hang a sign from my apartment window that said, "Hello, world! I'm back!" The world may not have missed me, but I missed me and was glad to feel like myself again. I felt like I'd just been released from prison. I felt free.

Chapter 8

Breaking Out of the Grief Bubble

When I planned a new life, I kept in mind all the years John and I spent together. I built upon the foundation of our love. Though I'll never completely recover from his death, I knew I could break out of the grief bubble and create a new life. I believe in the future and that the coming years of my life could be the most meaningful of all. Rather than being passive, I was proactive and determined to live a happy, meaningful life. Complete acceptance was my first step out of the grief bubble.

To move forward, I had to fully accept (or acknowledge, as some grief experts call it) the loss of my loved ones. Each loss was like a journey to a foreign land. I was somewhat familiar with this land, yet each territory—each death—was different. Even though I'm a realist, acceptance was hard for me, and the hardest part was losing John's support.

I was on my own.

Could I find my way through this new land? I wasn't sure. Two sentences rattled around in my head: "My loved ones are gone. I am alive." My deceased loved ones would want me to be happy and enjoy the remaining years of my life.

Life is for the Living

The time had come for recreation, new goals, and new meaning. Who would I be in my new life? What kind of life would I have?

The only way to find out was to break out of the bubble and get going and the idea scared me

To break out of the grief bubble, I listened to my self-talk and gauged my moods. I didn't do this occasionally; I did this constantly. This awareness helped me move forward on the healing path. Listening to myself also involved trusting my instincts, which I knew were good based on my past experiences.

I relied on my years with John to plan my new life.

John wasn't physically present, but I had a treasure trove of happy memories and funny memories too. Some people (who didn't know him well) thought John was quiet, and he could be quiet. I knew he was funny, gentle, caring, and kind. We traveled to many places together. I walked on the Great Wall of China with John, sailed on clipper ships, climbed pyramids in Mexico, rode cable cars in San Francisco, and more.

John was a role model for me, as well as for our daughters and grandchildren.

We had many things in common. Early in our marriage, we were interested in antiques and enjoyed browsing in antique shops and flea markets. I collected antique irons, a chronology of the Industrial Revolution, and we searched for them together. I had flat irons, charcoal irons, and kerosine irons. Kerosine irons could explode, so manufacturers stopped making them.

The iron collection was displayed in our kitchen. Every time I looked at a kerosine iron, a scene came to mind. I imagined a wife ironing her husband's shirt when the iron suddenly burst into flames, and there was a look of horror on her face. I could almost hear the wife's apology. "Sorry, dear, I blew up your shirt." I was thankful for my modern steam iron that didn't blow up.

John's expressions of love were sweet and memorable. When he was in Vietnam, he sent me pearls in a peanut can—a very

John thing to do. He enclosed a note on brown scrap paper with the pearls that said "I wuv you." (We joked about the words *love* and *wuv*.) Two years after John died, I found the note in a drawer, and it made John's death fresh again.

John's traits—generosity, kindness, honesty, and work ethic—became the framework of my new life.

Each trait was a girder, a source of support that held me up. Life started to look better. While my new life differed from the old, it contained some of the same things—hobbies, artistic endeavors, and volunteering. My life contained some new interests as well. I believed in the future, something American poet Robert Frost also believed.

When writing my research paper about Robert Frost for the Study Club, I discovered his life was filled with sorrow. His mother died of cancer. His beloved grandfather died. His first child, Elliott, died of cholera. His sixth child, Elinor, died. His adored sister Jeanie died. His daughter Marjorie died after childbirth. His son Carol died of suicide. The worst blow was when his wife, best friend, listener, and reviewer, died of a heart attack.

In his poem, "Bereft," Frost writes, "I had no one left but God."[29]

Despite his profound sorrow, Frost kept going and made the most of his remaining years. He became a United Nations ambassador and represented America around the world. Frost flew to Russia, met with Premier Nikita Khrushchev, and told him "Good fences make good neighbors," a line from his poem, "Mending Wall."[30] Though I wasn't a poet like Robert Frost, I learned from his experience and found strength in it.

---

29 Robert Frost, "Bereft," Robertfrost.org, accessed January 4, 2023, https://www.robertfrost.org/bereft.jsp.

30 Robert Frost, "Mending Wall," Robertfrost.org, accessed January 4, 2023, https://www.robertfrost.org/mending-wall.jsp.

My Formula

Because I'm a visual learner and list-maker, coming up with a life formula was natural for me. My formula was simple: Age + health + determination = healing.

Thanks to modern medicine, I survived endometrial cancer and open-heart surgery that involved a bypass. According to my primary care physician, I was in good health for my age. From now on, my health depended on maintenance. I had to watch for disturbing symptoms and report them to my doctor. The arthritis in my hands, hips, and back was painful, but not painful enough to keep me from doing what I wanted to do.

The urge to break out of the grief bubble became stronger. I stuck a toe out of my grief bubble as one would stick a toe into lake water to determine whether it was tepid or cold. I was tentative. Was life's temperature tepid, cold, or about right? I searched for positives in my life. After John died, my surviving daughter called me every night (a definite positive), and we had conversations about responding to grief.

We agreed on one point. Breaking out of the bubble required introspection, a process that could be happy, sad, confusing, and lengthy.

"You have to go inside to go outside," she summarized.

"I agree," I replied, "and I did it."

"I know you did," she said.

My daughter grieved for her older sister and was almost stuck in grief. Telling her story again and again was exhausting. When my daughter thought about the future, it was blank. Then, to her surprise, new experiences came into her life and changed it.

"I wasn't looking at the world through curtain sheers," she explained. "My life was moving forward."

My life also moved forward, and the future was uncertain. Nevertheless, I was willing to try new things and take risks. At the age of eighty-seven, failure isn't as intimidating as it used to be. Grief made me stronger. Grief made me a more resourceful person. Grief led to new experiences. Whether it was finances, car repairs, or home repairs, I took care of them all. I became Mrs. Reliable, someone I could count on to get the job done, and done on time.

Moving forward took willpower and mental power.

Intense Feelings

But when I broke out of the grief bubble, I hit a barrier—my intense feelings. If I wanted to continue to make progress, I would have to confront these feelings, name them, and make sense of them. Relief was one of the first emotions. I felt relieved because I experienced the stages of grief and left them behind. Then I felt guilty about feeling relieved.

Was I disrespecting my loved ones? No. I knew I had made progress and was walking toward the sunrise. I let go of many things to live a new life. Some of the articles and books I read made letting go sound too simple. There were too many do-it-yourself articles that summarized huge, and often expensive, projects in a couple of sentences.

My fictitious example: "Pour a cement slab, buy patio furniture and a grill. Have cookouts with your family."

Yeah right. A job like this could take days or weeks. Letting go could take years, and though it wasn't like pouring a cement slab, the weight of the process felt as heavy as cement.

Missing My Former Home

To let go, I faced reality, weighed my options, and did these things slowly. Letting go included saying goodbye to our Cape Cod house, one I really loved, and moving to a townhome in 2019.

During this time, after his second surgery for aortic dissection, John was in the ICU for weeks. I met with the supervising physician about John's dismissal.

"You have a three-story house," he began. "John can't go back there. I can't dismiss him until he has an address. Find somewhere for him to live, anywhere, an address I can use, and I'll dismiss him."

That was a tall order.

I contacted local nursing homes and senior living communities. None of them seemed right.

One retirement community looked like it would work, and I put our name on the waiting list. However, when I saw the apartment, I was disappointed. The apartment felt so cramped I didn't think one person could live there, let alone two. The bathroom wasn't handicapped accessible and needed to be totally renovated, a costly project. I removed our name from the list.

Instead of going to a retirement community, John went to a nursing home for six months while I built our townhome. In 2014 we moved into our Rochester townhome, and lived there for five years. It was wheelchair accessible, and I was pleased with the decorating after I finished it. I wanted the interior design to look like us, and it did. John loved our townhome, especially the great room, with its large windows that overlooked the garden and bird feeders.

Still, I missed the Cape Cod house we'd lived in for twenty years. We raised the twins there, had many happy times there, and the house sheltered us from blizzards and thunderstorms.

I missed the design of the house, the updated kitchen, home office, and front garden. The house and garden had looked like an illustration from a children's book. Cars used to stop to look at the Nearly Wild roses (a special variety), purple dianthus flowers (a hardy variety for a northern climate), and our tall pine tree.

I was at the grocery store when the tree had been planted at our Cape Cod house. When I returned home, I saw a small, crooked, limp pine tree in the front yard. The tree was so pathetic, a neighbor who walked by with his dog burst out laughing. Another neighbor drove by, saw the tree, and grinned. John wasn't thrilled with the tree when he came home from work.

"What's with the tree?" he asked.

"I don't know," I answered, "but it's not the one we ordered. It's Charlie Brown's Christmas tree. We paid big bucks for it. I'll call the nursery in the morning."

As promised, I called the nursery and explained my plight.

"You planted Charlie Brown's Christmas tree in my front yard," I began. "It's small, and crooked, and so pathetic the neighbors are laughing."

The nursery agreed to deliver and plant a replacement tree the next day. The second tree was straight and healthy. It grew into a tall, magnificent pine tree, suitable for a Christmas display in any town square.

Though it was a struggle, I let go of the tree, the garden, and the house. I also let go of a future with my daughter.

Letting Go

Helen and I wouldn't watch the twins grow together, discuss her career as a composite engineer, or swap stories about the twins. Helen wouldn't bake apple pies for us like she used to. She wouldn't be laughing at holiday dinners. A future without her was a colorless, vapid blank space, a place I didn't want to be. I let go of John's companionship.

John and I enjoyed each other, were honest with each other, and most importantly, listened to each other. After conversing with him for years about a wide range of topics—everything from saving whales, to changes in political parties, to child development—I didn't have anyone to talk to. The apartment was silent. I remembered past conversations and yearned to have new conversations with him.

I let go of family history carriers.

Everyone in the Hodgson family was a storyteller. One of the most interesting stories my father-in-law told was about a young family member who was left to homestead on some Minnesota land during the winter. The young man developed scurvy because food was limited. A traveler gave the relative an onion, and it contained enough vitamin C to stop the scurvy from getting worse. Family stories were history, and the generation that told them so eloquently was gone.

I let go of guilt.

Guilt was a corrosive emotion, like acid eating the soul. Though guilt could lead to good things, I considered it my enemy. More than that, guilt was a waste of energy. Instead of wasting time on guilt, I identified the positives in my life, and they were building blocks for the future. I had the basics: safe water, enough food, seasonal clothing, and shelter. I still had my education and life experience.

Holding On

I held on to happy memories.

Some of my best memories were of Christmas dinners at our house and relatives' houses. We had a live Christmas tree and decorated it with gift ornaments I received from nursery school students. The ornaments were charming: a tiny handmade sled, a photo of one of my students, and glittering stars. Each ornament made the tree unique. No other family in town had a tree like ours.

I held on to family traditions.

Before we ate Thanksgiving dinner, my father-in-law started a tradition of holding hands and saying, "God bless us everyone." After my father-in-law died, my brother-in-law continued this tradition. I want this custom to continue in the future, and time will tell if it will. In the meantime, I hold on to my spirituality and faith.

Dr. Katherine Piderman, Coordinator of Spirituality Research at Mayo Clinic, Rochester, defined spirituality in a way I understood: "Spirituality is an opportunity to experience life at the deepest level. It gives you a way to approach each day with wonder and gratitude, grace and generosity, meaning and purpose."[31] Piderman uses this definition with patients who participate in the Hear My Voice program, a storytelling, remembrance, and thoughtful program for hospice patients. This program helps participants answer I-wish-I-knew and I-wish-I'd-told thoughts.

In my confused state, I wondered if church members would respond to my daughter's death and John's death. Church members didn't just respond, they rallied. One couple gave us a book they read after their son had died.

"It helped us and may help you," my friend said.

The Caring Committee sent me cards for years after John died. Support from my church congregation kept me going.

I held on to love.

Not many couples were as close as we were. John's death didn't quell my love; I loved him more than ever. I often dreamed about John. In my dreams, we were on a trip and having fun together. Several times I dreamed we were lost and woke up

---

31 Katherine Piderman, quoted in Dana Sparks, "Mayo Mindfulness: Defining Spirituality," Mayo Clinic News Network, June 19, 2019, https://newsnetwork. mayoclinic.org/discussion/mayo-mindfulness-defining-spirituality-2/.

suddenly. My wish-fulfillment dreams were signs that I wished John were still alive.

Joy of Doodle Art

I was glad John knew about my doodling book before he died. The simple illustrations I drew for the book, *Grief Doodling: Bringing Back Your Smiles*, evolved into personal, colorful art. When I worked on a doodle art picture, I felt like an invisible hand was guiding me. My doodle art surprised my daughter and surprised me. Every picture was a surprise.

When I started a picture, I never knew how it would turn out. Pictures I thought would be good were not, and pictures I thought would be awful were good.

My pictures were a riot of color because I enjoyed using color in surprising ways. A yellow sky. Purple tree trunks. Red Valentine flowers. The color choices I made surprised me. Weeks after John died, I ordered a round table online, an impulsive thing to do. I did it anyway. I positioned the table in the cetner of the room.

Hmm, that's a good place for the table, I thought to myself. *Good light from both windows and ideal for creating doodle art.*

Maybe ordering a table wasn't so crazy after all. Maybe my subconscious was telling me to move forward with life.

John's bedroom, formerly a place of sadness, became a place of joy, and the walls are covered with framed doodle art. People who visited my studio gasped in surprise.

"What a wonderful room!" one exclaimed.

"Your pictures make me happy," another said.

"You did all these?" a third visitor inquired.

Yes, I did them all. Doodle art was my new occupation.

Charter House sent out a notice asking for artists to exhibit their work in the Parkside Gallery. I contacted the activities director and said I would be willing to participate. I invited her to my apartment to see my work. She accepted my invitation, approved the pictures, counted them, and told me when the group display would open.

I needed more frames to exhibit my art. I ordered twenty white, double-matted frames from Amazon. The frames were perfect, so I ordered ten more. When I typed the numeral "ten" on the order form, Amazon refused to accept it. I typed the numeral "ten" again, and Amazon wouldn't accept it. It was time to call customer support.

A pleasant-sounding woman answered the phone, and I explained my predicament.

"Give me a minute to check your order," she said.

A couple of minutes later, she told me the manufacturer was having problems (probably supply chain problems), and the frames weren't available.

"But my artwork is going to be in a show, and I need ten more frames," I explained.

"Sorry, my bad," she replied.

"Are you saying I need to order substitute frames?" I inquired.

"Yes."

"Okay, I'll do that."

I went online again, found some small blue frames, and ordered them. The next day, my original order of twenty frames arrived. The day after, my blue substitute frames arrived. The day after that, my order of ten frames arrived. I felt like I was living a scene from the *I Love Lucy* show. In one episode, Lucy worked in a chocolate factory and the candy kept coming on the assembly line. To keep up with the line, she stuffed chocolates into her mouth.

Well, like Lucy's experience, the frames kept coming. So many frames arrived, the delivery person opened my apartment door and set the box in the front hall. At least I had enough frames for the art exhibit. The activities director hung the doodle art, and I helped her with placement decisions. People who walked by didn't know I was the artist, and I listened to their comments.

Two housekeepers: "Wow, look at those colors!"

A nurse: "These pictures are so happy!"

Charter House resident: "Oh, these are so cute!"

Another Charter House resident stopped and studied each picture. We chatted a bit, and I could tell she was an artist. I shared with her some of the comments I'd overheard. When I mentioned the comment about the pictures looking "cute," she shook her head in disagreement.

"These pictures aren't cute," she declared firmly. "You went inside and found joy."

And she was right. I went inside with my doodle art to go outside and break out of the grief bubble. I didn't just break out, I burst out.

I gave talks to community groups about grief doodling. I gave tours of my studio and demonstrated techniques. I gave workshops about doodle art and the techniques I used. I gave a doodle art workshop at the Rochester Art Center. I made additions and corrections to my writing in my sleep. Once I became engrossed in doodle art, I planned pictures in my sleep.

From Sadness to Joy

If doodle art helped me, I thought it could help others. I wrote and illustrated *Grief Doodling: Bringing Back Your Smiles*. Originally intended for tweens and teens, grief experts have said the book is for all ages. The book received several awards, and I was thrilled. Doodle art was more than self-care. For me, doodle art was a way to change pain into joy. My doodle art pictures radiated happiness because I was happy.

As I approached the end of my life, I had a new life. I

became a working doodle artist and updated my business card to read "Harriet Hodgson, Health/Wellness Author, Speaker, and Doodle Artist." My life was more than okay. I had a productive, meaningful, and happy life, one I created for myself.

Breaking out of the grief bubble made me feel more secure. I shared my grief story with others and encouraged them to share theirs. Humans have been telling stories ever since they gathered around fire for warmth. Many grief experts say telling stories can foster healing. The meaning of grief begins and ends with the stories we tell, according to David Kessler.[32]

Of his son's death, Kessler writes: "I need to be of service and keep my own pain moving."[33] I had a similar thought after I broke out of the grief bubble. To keep my pain moving and to make my life meaningful, I made the most important decision of my life. I chose happiness instead of sadness.

Happy Thoughts

Happiness was a hot topic and continues to be a hot topic. Dr. Amit Sood thinks happiness can be created with conscious, constant effort. "Research shows that up to 50 percent of our happiness depends on our conscious choices that, with time, become enduring habits," Sood notes.[34]

He goes on to say there are four kinds of resilience: physical, cognitive, emotional, and spiritual. Physical resilience means being strong and healthy. Emotional resilience means staying focused when stressed. Emotional resilience means having positive feelings. Spiritual resilience means having higher meaning and a

---

32 Kessler, *Finding Meaning*, 51.

33 Kessler, *Finding Meaning*, 10.

34 Amit Sood, *The Mayo Clinic Handbook for Happiness: A Four-Step Plan for Resilient Living* (New York: Hachette Books, 2015), 25.

selfless perspective.[35] This made me reflect on my own resilience and how it had grown.

My definition of happiness is mine alone, as unique as my thumbprint, as unique as my grief. For me, happiness means a busy mind, attainable goals, creative endeavors (doodle art, writing, cooking, singing), and helping others. Quiet time, and having time to think creatively, also made me happy.

Everyone has their own definition of happiness. Skiing was not an activity on my happiness chart, for example. I figured if I were supposed to ski, God, my Higher Power, or Spirit of Life would have attached skis to my feet. The idea of shooting down a mountain at breakneck speed doesn't appeal to me; it terrifies me. I realized I could find happiness in things I used to enjoy, and new things.

Finding unique moments in a day was easy because I saw everything through an art lens. A unique photo made me ask, "How could I doodle that?" An eye-catching color made me wonder, "Is that dark yellow or ocher?" A stunning floral bouquet made me stop, evaluate the design, and look at the centers of the flowers. I was surrounded by art every day.

Because I was on constant sensory alert, using one sensory system at a time was harder. I smelled the scent of spring, identified the pitch of things from car horns to the church elevator, and savored the taste of beef burgundy, one of my favorite meals I've ever prepared. Separating the senses was tricky but not impossible. I was able to do this when I focused my thoughts.

Finding interesting details was automatic for me. I found details all the time—a crooked chair leg, the stamens of a flower, a pink-and-blue-striped sky at sunset. To foster happiness, I ramped up my observation of details. I was, and continue to be,

35 Sood, *Handbook for Happiness*, 38–39.

a detail person. My personal story was chock full of details, and I shared my grief story with others who were bereaved.

The Comfort of Linking Objects

Giving away linking objects were part of my story. Linking objects are things that belong to the deceased person, such as a watch, a bread knife, woodworking tools, and more. As soon as he died, I slipped John's wedding ring on my finger. Wearing the ring made me feel like John was still with me. I touched the ring and remembered the years we shared. Wearing John's ring comforts me every day.

Linking objects could comfort other family members. I gave John's black leather medical bag with gold letters on the side that read, "C. John Hodgson, MD," to my grandson.

When my grandson looked at the contents of the bag, he said, "You don't see these things anymore." The bag contained a knee hammer, a dated stethoscope, and other medical tools. Looking inside the bag was looking at medical history.

I gave my daughter the handcrafted mug John used to keep pencils and pens in when he was a child. The relief on the outside of the mug depicted the story of Little Red Riding Hood. I also gave my daughter John's winter Air Force coat. The coat was about forty years old, had a broken zipper, and needed to be dry-cleaned. My daughter wears her father's coat when she plows snow. The coat keeps her warm and makes her feel close to her dad. She thought about having the coat cleaned but changed her mind.

"I didn't want to wash Dad off," she explained. I think her explanation is wonderful.

I found more of John's linking objects, including three NASA passes from the days when he was a flight surgeon at NASA

Houston. Without the passes, John wouldn't have been admitted to mission control. The passes were part of John's history and our family history. This history needed to be shared. I gave a NASA pass to my daughter and the twins.

Breaking out of the grief bubble didn't mean I forgot my loved ones. Every day, I thought about them and remembered them with "action memorials," the words I used to explain my actions. The idea for the memorials came from Dr. Therese A. Rando, and I'm grateful for it. One way to keep a loved one in your life, Rando writes, is to identify with the person. "It is a way in which you can keep him with you."[36]

How could I keep my loved ones close? I thought about the qualities Helen, my father-in-law, my brother, the twins' father, and John exhibited. Each one had special qualities, and I chose one quality that represented each of them. Helen's humor. My father-in-law's ethics. My brother's love of reading. The twins' father's love of nature. John's love of medicine.

In memory of my daughter, I decided to laugh more.

The first laugh happened in a Twin Cites restaurant. A year after Helen died, John and I took our youngest daughter out to dinner. While we waited for our food to arrive, we swapped stories about our trip to London and the Isle of Man. The stories became funnier and funnier, and our laughter got louder and louder, so loud I thought we'd be thrown out of the restaurant. I hadn't laughed since Helen died, and my laughter was as rusty as an old hinge.

As laughter poured out of my body, I said to myself, "Helen, these laughs are dedicated to you."

Our dinners arrived, and the food was as delicious as we

---

36 Rando, *How to Go On Living*, 43.

expected. I had almost decided to skip dessert when the waiter set a dish of crème brûlée at my place.

"This is for you," he explained. "No charge."

I was flabbergasted. Why had the waiter given me a free dessert? Though I never answered the question, several ideas came to mind.

Perhaps the waiter enjoyed seeing a family laugh together. Perhaps he enjoyed seeing my belly laughs. Perhaps he was just being kind. I wrote an article about the experience titled "Belly Laughs and Crème Brûlée." I continue to dedicate belly laughs, and regular laughs, to Helen. With each laugh I say to myself, "Helen, here's another one for you."

Action Memorials

I decided to do something in memory of my departed loved ones, starting with my father-in-law. My father-in-law was one of the most ethical people I'd ever known. Nothing kept Dad from doing the right thing. When it came to medical decisions, he researched the condition, thought about it, and took action. When it came to family, he did the right thing. I vowed to do the right thing in his memory.

This involved saying no, which had been difficult in the past. After Dad died, I said no easily in his memory. Even better, I didn't feel guilty about this response.

In memory of my brother, I became more involved with books and reading. We had a large library of books in our house. Before John and I moved into our townhome, I had donated dozens of books to the Friends of the Library bookstore. I volunteered at the store and served as secretary of the group until I became John's caregiver. I also donated some of the books I published to the public library.

In memory of the twins' father, I became acutely aware of

nature. He loved to fish on the Mississippi River. Water skiing was invented in Lake City, a small town on the Mississippi. Whenever I heard boating or fishing stories, I thought about my former son-in-law. Observing nature restored my soul.

In memory of John, I stayed connected to medicine. John loved being a specialist in aviation and aerospace medicine. He enjoyed using his graduate degree in public health. As soon as I heard about the invasion in Ukraine, I donated to medical organizations that were already there or on the border. Donating to these organizations made me feel like I continued John's medical practice. I also stayed in touch with members of the aviation and aerospace community.

Action memorials linked me to my loved ones every day. Whether small or significant, these actions kept my loved ones alive in my mind. The actions made my loved ones real in small and significant ways. Each departed loved one contributed to family history. I didn't want to forget my loved ones, and I didn't want family members to forget them.

Breaking out of the grief bubble made me more aware of my life and where I was headed. Was I on track? Was I doing well? I took a mental snapshot of an ordinary day. First, I reviewed my activities.

Writing and reading were a part of every day, which was good. Since I loved to bake, some days I made muffins or cookies, which was not so good.

"Passes the lips, goes straight to the hips," I reminded myself.

As much as I loved to bake, I limited this activity. I also limited my food intake to 1,200 calories a day, give or take a few.

Next, I thought about things I would stop doing. John had subscribed to many magazines, and I canceled his subscriptions. He had donated to Dartmouth College, and since John was no longer alive, I stopped the donations. I canceled his memberships in several organizations. Each cancellation proved I accepted John's death and was moving forward on my healing path.

Finally, I looked at the new things I added to an ordinary day, and speaking was one of them, something I enjoyed. I received more invitations to speak and to give more doodling workshops, and I accepted them. Doodle art was an especially joyful experience for me, and workshop participants picked up on my joy.

Planning the Future While Staying Present

Grief taught me that preparing for my own death was a gift for loved ones. If I plan well, my loved ones will have less to do after I die. Equally important, they will understand my wishes. I bought two file cabinets and filed important documents. I taped explanatory labels—such as photo albums, family history, and tax information—to the cupboards. I wrote my own obituary and thought it was good.

I shared important information with my youngest daughter since she would be responsible for my burial and legal and financial arrangements. We had frank discussions, and she knew what I wanted. These discussions brought us closer than we had ever been. We went on two cruises together, one on the lower Mississippi River, and one on the Snake and Columbia Rivers. We had fun and laughed like crazy.

As much as I enjoyed these cruises, I didn't need special events to appreciate the ordinary days of my life. My schedule, activities, and interests made the days of the week similar, yet each day was special. Every new day, and every breath I took, was a gift. Whether they were ordinary or not, I wanted to savor these gifts. Again, I realized ordinary days and things I often took for granted, were extraordinary.

My rich life was about to become richer.

I read Katrina Kenison's book, *The Gift of an Ordinary Day*. Her book confirmed some of my ideas and made me feel better about life in general. "Real life is just where we are, in this moment, and the only mistake we've made so far has been not to pause long enough or often enough to realize that even this odd in-between time is precious, fleeting, and worthy of our attention," Kenison writes.[37]

Her words reminded me to stop and smell the flowers, as the saying goes. These words altered my thoughts, actions, and decision-making.

Some of my plans faded away and others came true. Even though nothing special was planned, I could step up to the adventure of my life. Determining the direction of the adventure was up to me. Many changes awaited me. While I couldn't predict changes, I knew they might include heart problems, vision problems (I have early macular degeneration), and God forbid, memory problems. So far, my brain is functioning well, and I attribute this to writing and the research I did for my books.

Becoming a widow and suffering multiple losses taught me a great deal about grief. My opinions could change in the future. I continue to learn about grief, which brought me back to today and what I might make of it. Each day is filled with possibilities. After years of grief, after crying an ocean of tears, I finally broke out of the grief bubble.

Determination helped me do it. I had happy memories, family traditions, spirituality, religion, and love. I let go of the things I needed to. Choosing happiness was the most important decision I've ever made. I could be, and vowed to be, a creative survivor of grief. However long it might be, I will live the best life I can, one I've created for myself. I vow to make good things from grief.

---

37 Katrina Kenison, *The Gift of an Ordinary Day: A Mother's Memoir* (New York: Grand Central Publishing, 2009), 89–90.

Chapter 9

Making Good Things from Grief

When John died, I didn't know how to go on living. Rather than existing, I wanted to flourish and savor life. That meant setting goals, working for them, and reaching them. I wanted my living loved ones—and John—to be proud of me. Creating a new life took gumption, and I had it. Grief could have a better outcome if I let it. I could learn from grief and use my experience to help others.

Judy Tatelbaum, author of *The Courage to Grieve*, thinks grieving people need to make good from their grief. "Making our grief meaningful can be an antidote to despair and suffering as well as the stepping stone to personal growth and achievement," she explains.[38] Her words strengthened my resolve. I found many ways to make good from grief—some traditional, some nontraditional, and some that were new for me.

My goals were to share the talents I'd been given, be grateful for what I had, live mindfully, adapt to life, and focus on the positives. The old caregiving to-do list was replaced by a new to-do list. The first two items on my list: "Live the best life" and "Be happy." I was the "executive" in charge of my happiness, and it began with writing more books and giving talks and workshops about grief.

38 Judy Tatelbaum, *The Courage to Grieve: The Classic Guide to Creative Living, Recovery, and Growth Through Grief* (New York: HarperCollins, 2009), 139.

John often said I was low maintenance, not the kind of person who needed flashy stuff to be happy. For me, happiness is sitting in my favorite chair, which is probably forty years old, with a cup of coffee within reach and an engrossing book in my hands. Happiness means sitting on a bench in the park across the street and doing nothing. Silence doesn't bother me.

Life was an adventure, and I wondered what was around the next corner. I wanted to live life to the fullest. Would life disappoint me or surprise me?

Writing Career

During my forty-five-year career as a freelance author, I wrote forty-five books. The books didn't write themselves. My writing career hinged on research and strong work habits. I started typing in the basement near the furnace. Then I graduated to a personal computer and workstation. Tractor printers were slow, and mine was so slow that I would start it, go to the grocery store, and the printer would still be going by the time I got home. I was excited when I graduated to a home office and bought an inkjet printer. Having a new printer and place to write made writing easier.

Many people have asked me if *Winning* would be my last book. "I'm not sure," I answered, "because I never know when an idea will strike." I've had several ideas for new books and haven't decided whether I will pursue them. This decision depends on book sales and my health. If I'm being honest with myself, I hope I'll write another book because I have more things to say, and my mind is still working.

Hope was important for both my future and my mental health. I had hope for my books, my family, and my life. My mother felt she lived at the best time. I adopted her attitude and acted on it. No matter what was going on in the world, or in my corner of the world, I celebrated life. I looked to the future with hope.

As Emily Dickinson wrote in one of her poems, "Hope is the thing with feathers that perches in the soul."[39] Though I occasionally faltered, I followed the star of hope. This decision required emotional maturity—the willingness to identify feelings, let myself feel them, and express them. I evaluated my emotional maturity. Prior to the multiple losses I experienced, I thought I was mature. After multiple losses, however, my emotional maturity slipped. To get back on track, I lived more mindfully, a practice that took constant and concentrated effort.

Living Mindfully

An article by Rachel Sharpe, "Mindful Living: 16 Ways to Live Mindfully in 2022," has some good suggestions. Cooking your own meals and eating slowly are two of them.[40] I fixed my own meals and enjoyed them, but I didn't eat slowly; I ate rapidly. Food tasted differently when John wasn't sitting across the table from me. I ate quickly just to get it over with, then wiped the counters and washed the dishes. I hoped to become a slower, more appreciative eater in the future.

Looking up when walking is another of Sharpe's ideas.[41] Though I usually looked up to steady my gait, I looked down and focused on small details, such as a dandelion growing out of a crack in the sidewalk. Seeing small details in a big picture helped me live mindfully. Life outside my apartment windows also helped me practice mindful living.

What did I see? I saw cars stopped for red lights, giant rain

---

39 Emily Dickinson, "Hope is the Thing with Feathers" *The Complete Poems* (New York: Little, Brown, 1924), 19.

40 Rachel Sharpe, "Mindful Living: 16 Ways to Live Mindfully in 2022," Declutter the Mind, September 22, 2020, https://declutterthemind.com/blog/mindful-living/.

41 Ibid.

puddles, workers mowing lawns or buzzing snowplows, people hurrying to work, helicopters landing on the Methodist Hospital helipad, flocks of crows flying by, people on bikes, Christmas trees decorated with lights, and insects clinging to windowpanes. The scene from my window was filled with glorious, colorful images.

Living mindfully meant having good habits. Every morning I made my bed. Dirty dishes went straight into the dishwasher. Anything that needed to be washed by hand was washed immediately. I thought a cluttered apartment was an indication of a cluttered mind, so I tidied my apartment regularly. Neat place, neat mind.

A visitor came to see my apartment. After she left, she told family members, "Harriet is very organized."

And I was organized. The places that were supposed to be messy were messy—my doodle art supplies, my office filled with seemingly random papers, the counter where I sorted mail. All were messy. That was okay with me. Messy places were evidence of works in progress and the sign of a busy mind. My mind was busy all the time.

Sharpe's other ideas for mindful living—getting up early, being kind, listening attentively—were already part of my life.[42] Friends couldn't believe I got up at four thirty in the morning, but that was my body's rhythm. Trying to change this rhythm made no sense. Ever since we were little kids, my brother and I were early risers. Getting up at five in the morning was normal for kids like us.

One Fourth of July when we were children, my brother had opened his bedroom window at five in the morning, stuck his trumpet into the air, and played patriotic songs. Neighbors didn't

---

42 Sharpe, "Mindful Living."

want to hear the national anthem, "America," or "My Country 'Tis of Thee" at the crack of dawn. Around eight o'clock, complaint calls from neighbors began to come in, and my parents were embarrassed.

"We never heard a sound," my mother said.

Really?

My brother's bedroom had been next to my parents' bedroom, and I was sure they'd heard his trumpet music. I felt my mother and father were being disingenuous. But Mom and Dad wanted to get along with our neighbors, so they stuck to their story. They said they were sound asleep and never heard a note. This story still makes me smile. Mindful living focuses on the present but, at the time, I was mindfully aware of my brother's love of the trumpet.

Adaptation was part of my decision to live mindfully. I was aware of my friends' mood changes, strangers' feelings, and people's body language. The decision to live mindfully made me acutely aware of these signs, and my communication skills improved. One friend told me I had a creative mind. I thought she was really commenting about communication.

Usually I adapted to change well, but having an unreliable Internet connection threw me for a loop. I lived in a corner unit, and though the building didn't have steel beams, it had massive cement beams that interfered with Wi-Fi. For two long weeks, I was without reliable Internet service. I called the Charter House tech support person, and he installed a new Wi-Fi connection in the hallway. It didn't work as well as the old connection, so he reinstalled the old connection.

The technician was patient and kind. He brought his personal laptop to my apartment and tested the signal by moving from room to room. The signal was still weak. My part-time job depended on reliable Internet. Mayo Clinic planned to install a new, updated system, but that hadn't happened because of the supply chain problems.

"I guess swearing doesn't work," I told the technician.

"Guess not," he chuckled.

I ordered a Wi-Fi booster from Amazon, but that didn't work either. At this rate, I would need therapy. Finally, I switched to another provider and had a reliable Internet connection. Thank goodness!

Living mindfully meant renewing my purpose. My purpose was the same: to write books that helped others. I added doodle art to this purpose. In my mind, writing and art were good outcomes of grief. These pursuits connected me with the outside world. I met new people and made new friends, two things that might not have happened without renewed purpose.

Donating and Volunteering

I continue to donate to the Doctors Mayo Society in honor of John's love for medicine and life. The check represents both of our lives. However, I cried when I wrote the check, and that was okay. Though my signature is on the check, the money is from John as well.

Donating money to my church also made good things from grief. After John died, I sent a check to the church and asked that the money go into the general fund. I donated three doodle art pictures to the church auction and displayed artwork in the lobby. The church secretary hung the doodle art pictures on a special track (a great idea), and the display looked as I had imagined.

Afterward, a member of the congregation came up to me and said, "It's nice to have some color here." No doubt about it, my pictures almost burst with color.

Because I cared about books and reading, I donated money to

the public library. John's newspaper obituary suggested memorials to the library. I received a list of donors and thanked each one via email. My library connections were more than donations. I gave a grief doodling workshop to patrons and added a copy of my latest book to the children's collection.

The best way to make good from grief was to give myself away. Instead of buying cards, I created doodle art greetings for people. At the bottom of one picture, I printed "Be a Blessing," words that summarized my friend's life. I donated four framed doodle art pictures to Charter House and sixteen pictures to a fundraiser for residents in need.

When I could, and when I was asked, I mentored other writers. I also gave books to friends, colleagues, and community contacts.

Volunteering was another way I gave myself away. I used to be active in Zumbro Valley Medical Society Alliance (ZVMSA), an organization for spouses and partners of physicians, researchers, and other health care professionals. I stopped volunteering when John's health failed. After he died, I returned to volunteering, and ZVMSA made *Grief Doodling* its health outreach project.

Every school counselor and social worker in the Rochester Public Schools received a copy of the book. ZVMSA also gave books to public health nurses, and I gave workshops to county public health departments, school districts, and the local chapter of the Boys & Girls Club. *Grief Doodling* helped more people than I'd ever imagined.

I arranged for a grove of trees to be planted in memory of John. The US National Forest program plants trees in memory of loved ones and beloved pets in honor of significant events, and to conserve land destroyed by forest fires, insects, and national disasters. "Every tree is a living legacy—a gift which will grow stronger year after year—and a unique way to express your feelings," the website says.[43] Planting a grove of trees was a gift to my daughter, and she received a certificate of planting. The gesture touched her deeply.

"There's an odd synergism in it," she explained. "It reminded me of the circle of life and new life in the face of death. The trees will probably outlast me."

Planting the trees made me think of John's amazing life.

The Blessings of Laughter

Laughter helped me make good from grief. Thanks to my grief work and the passage of time, my spontaneous laughter is back. Laughing brought back a treasured memory from my years as my mother's caregiver in the 1980s. Though Mom had vascular dementia, it didn't prevent her from enjoying lunch at a restaurant and getting out. Mom and I had gone shopping together. When we left the shopping center, I saw a large brown dog sitting in a car. The dog had its two front paws on the steering wheel. "Look, Mom, a driving dog!" I exclaimed.

Mom looked at the dog and laughed like she hadn't laughed in months. She turned away briefly, as if she couldn't believe her eyes, then looked back at the car. The dog's paws were still on the steering wheel.

"He really is a driving dog!" she exclaimed and laughed some more. Her laughter had lingered in the air like a robin's song. Mom never laughed like that again, yet it is one of my happiest memories of her.

Speaking at Events

Making good from grief meant giving talks to community

---

43 "Trees Make Wonderful Gifts," The Trees Remember, accessed December 15, 2022, https://thetreesremember.com/.

groups. Talking about painful experiences and offering hope wasn't easy. Right after my mother passed away, I gave a talk to Catholic nuns about caring for people with dementia. At the end of my talk, I quoted my mother's comment about living at the best time.

"What would happen if we all thought we were living at the best time?" I asked. "How could we change things?"

Tears trickled down my face as I spoke these sentences. I wondered if I had made a fool of myself and shared this concern with a friend.

"Don't worry," she replied. "I heard all about it and the nuns loved it."

What a dear friend.

My recent talks have been varied, some about grief doodling, others about affirmation writing, and even more about coping with feelings. These actions—giving talks, planting a grove of trees in memory of John, volunteering, and donating to health organizations—improved my life. I hoped they would improve the lives of others as well.

When Grief Surprised Me

On May 16, 2022, there was a lunar eclipse. Television news talked about the forthcoming eclipse, when it would happen, and how it would look. I remembered John's dream of going to the moon. He ordered a map of the moon from the Smithsonian Institution, and we were probably the only family in Rochester that had one. The map was huge. Since we couldn't afford to have it framed, we stored the map in the furnace room.

I didn't see the entire eclipse because I'd been upset. Once I had my feelings under control, I went to a window in my art studio and gazed at the moon. Most of it was black, but some dark red was still visible. I hadn't missed the entire eclipse, and it was amazing.

I thought of my beloved John, the dreamer, the specialist in aerospace and aviation medicine, and charter member of the NASA flight surgeons. The eclipse activated my grief, and I cried. I thought of the moon map that was stored in the basement. Unfortunately, a mouse had wiggled its way into the furnace room and eaten the edges. I threw the map away before we moved into our apartment.

Fighting Ageism

Taking chances was another way I made good things from grief. I ramped up my book marketing. At the suggestion of my publisher, I entered my books in contests. Most contests had a reader's fee. If I didn't win, my money was lost. Thankfully, many of my books won awards. I could still write and deliver, and I was grateful for that. Because I was a victim of ageism, I decided to fight ageism when necessary. Ageism is prejudice or discrimination of people based on age. Though ageism is usually associated with older adults, young people can also be victims of a "he-is-too-young-to-know-anything" notion. In my late fifties, I experienced ageism when I participated in a study about heart function and aging. How ironic.

As directed, I had reported to the nurse, who told me to walk down the hall as quickly as possible.

"Do you see the marker at the end of the hall?" she asked in a tone that sounded like she was speaking to a two-year-old. "Walk down to the marker, turn around, and come back. Do you understand?"

Yes, I understood and wanted to smack her. I was older, not stupid.

The nurse didn't know I was on a walking program. I walked down the hall at a good clip, avoided one nurse and one doctor, turned around, and raced back to my starting point.

"That was good," the nurse commented in a surprised voice.

I didn't confront her on the ageism issue. Today, my response would be different.

There are many examples of ageism. I heard too many ageism jokes that weren't funny. Almost every week, television and print media contained stories about older adults being swindled out of their money. One time, I received a call from a man who pretended to be my grandson.

"Hi, Grandma," he began. "How are you doing?"

The man's voice sounded older than my grandson's voice.

"I'm in jail and need bail money," the man said.

He told me to deliver the money to a specific location. It all sounded fishy to me.

"Peter, you don't sound like yourself today," I commented.

The caller hung up immediately.

To be on the safe side, I called the Mayo Clinic Medical School secretary. "I'm Peter's grandmother. Did he come to school today?" I asked.

"Yes, and he's in class now," she replied.

I described the scam call, and she was familiar with it. I notified the Rochester Police about the scam. The person I talked with wasn't surprised and said the department had received dozens of reports. I wanted to call the scammer back and tell him to get a real job.

Ageism can be present in healthcare settings. Uninformed staff may think depression comes with getting older, which is a false belief. Ageism causes higher rates of illness, higher healthcare spending, poverty, and lower life expectancy. For some, ageism is downright dangerous.[44]

Making a Difference

I am only one person, yet I can make a difference. Rather than concealing my age, I am forthright. When health care professionals ask for my date of birth, I tell them and add, "I'm eighty-seven years old and still working."

Their replies have been interesting:

"Wow!"

"You don't look it."

"Good for you!"

"That is amazing."

"You're eighty-seven years old?"

Many friends say I don't look my age. That's nice to hear, but my body knows my age, something my father-in-law understood. Dad used to say he could feel every rock he walked on, a comment I didn't understand at the time but understand now. I persevered with the age issue. When friends asked me what I was doing, I said I was writing books, articles, and a column for an online magazine.

This news pleased some people, shocked others, and several friends thought I was doing too much. Their "too much" wasn't my "too much."

I participated in a radio conference about aging hosted by a friend from the past, Dr. Roger Landry. His program, "Masterpiece," was established in 1999 to change the perception of aging and gather data on the topic. He sent me questions before

44 Zawn Villines, "What is Ageism, and How Does It Affect Health?" Medical News Today, November 3, 2021, https://www.medicalnewstoday.com/articles/ageism.

we recorded the program. Dr. Landry was an excellent host, and I thought the interview went well.

"I can tell you've done this before," Dr. Landry said. "You're a natural. You're a national treasure."

National treasure or not, I feel my age. Things that didn't hurt before are starting to hurt. I describe myself as "creaky." Having a pig valve in my heart and two other leaking valves is a challenge. I monitor my health and stay in touch with my primary care physician. With good medical care and determination, I can celebrate more birthdays.

One-Sentence Compliments

Giving people one-sentence compliments, something I'd started long ago, was another way to make good things from grief. Of course, my compliments were genuine.

I monitor the pitch of my voice because a higher pitch, or a sentence that ends on a higher pitch, can sound like a question. I observe body language and signs of tension: a stiff mouth, shaking foot, or nervous hand gestures such as drumming fingers on a table. My short compliments are easy to remember, and the recipients enjoy them.

"You must be a patient person," I said to a workman.

"I try to be patient," he answered with a smile.

Though I used this compliment several times, I didn't over-use it.

"Thank you for the gift of listening," was another compliment I gave to others, and some were startled. "We live in a noisy, fast-paced world," I explained, "and it's hard to listen attentively. You do."

I continue to give one-sentence compliments to friends and strangers. Doing this is a way to help others and, from my viewpoint, a way of sharing positive thoughts. This makes me feel good inside.

Stepping Out of My Comfort Zone

Stepping out of my comfort zone is another positive approach, and I'm doing it more often. Exploring a new writing genre helped me make good from grief. Writing creative nonfiction was a huge step out of my comfort zone. Thousands of words rattled around in my mind, and adjusting to the genre took weeks. I returned to the earlier chapters I wrote, read them aloud, edited them, and changed them. Writing creative nonfiction was a new and joyful experience.

Getting rid of stuff wasn't joyful. Before we moved into our Charter House apartment, I gave away furniture, tools, kitchen supplies, clothes, books, gadgets, and more. Goodwill received most of our donations. Because I cleaned out our townhome in a rush, I gave away things that I wished I had kept. Oh well. I didn't need any more stuff. My apartment was attractive and homey.

Getting a website was a step out of my comfort zone. Since I didn't know squat about website design, my talented granddaughter designed it. My blog is part of my website, and monthly electronic newsletters are posted on it. Writing short newsletters took more than I imagined. I started with the headings: From My Window (personal news), Book Business (current writing projects, updates, release dates), Reviews, and the Quote of the Month.

The responses to my newsletter were encouraging. Several readers asked me to include more personal information, and I did. As soon as I finished one newsletter, I worked on the next. With each issue, writing the electronic newsletter became easier.

Adding personal news and photos made readers feel like they knew me. (And some did.)

I included an article about being the keynote speaker for the Elder Network fundraiser at the International Event Center in the fall of 2022. Though I'd given many talks and workshops, I had some reservations. Speaking while people were finishing dinner was dicey. My challenge was to keep them awake. Or, as a friend noted, "You stand and deliver."

An experienced speaker, I knew I could deliver, but two days before the event I had surgery for a cancerous growth. The bandage on my hairline was as large as a golf ball. The next day, following the doctor's advice, I replaced the protruding bandage with a flat, skin-colored bandage. Before I left for the event center, I combed my bangs over the bandage. Would listeners be distracted by the bandage?

Rather than standing at the podium, I wore a clip-on microphone and circulated among the tables as I spoke. Nobody seemed to notice the bandage. Audience members were attentive and gave me a hearty round of applause at the end of my talk.

"You're a natural," one said as I walked by.

My Bucket List

I enjoyed speaking to groups, and future talks were on my bucket list. Author Judith Viorst describes her bucket list in *Nearing Ninety*, a collection of wise, witty, laugh-aloud poems. Viorst begins by sharing things that are not on her bucket list. Fearlessly riding a camel across desert sands isn't on the list, nor is being the oldest student at Harvard Medical School. Viorst's "yay" and "nay" bucket lists made me chuckle.[45]

---

45 Judith Viorst, *Nearing Ninety: And Other Comedies of Late Life* (New York: Simon & Schuster, 2019).

I decided to make my own list and, like Viorst, listed the negatives first. Taking a computer science course wasn't on my list. Going to culinary school wasn't on my list, though the prospect sounded interesting. For sure, becoming a decathlon champion wasn't on my list. Getting tattoos on my aging skin wasn't on my list. Going to Las Vegas and gambling with my hard-earned money wasn't on my list either.

What is on my list?

Taking another trip with my daughter is a possibility. Whether or not I do this depends on my health. Writing another book is definitely a possibility. I love to write and want to keep doing it. Giving workshops about grief doodling and general doodling is another possibility. I can't predict the future and might do something very out of character. Thinking about my bucket list makes me think about my legacy.

When family members recall my life, I hope they'll say I lived it well. Being remembered as a creative person would be nice too. I hope family members will tell funny stories about my twenty-three years of caregiving, my writing career, and my new career as a doodle artist. Despite the daunting odds, I hope family members will say I renewed myself.

My circle of life is nearly complete.

The circle may well be humanity's best invention. Circles appear in ancient artwork and pottery. You've read about my ensō circles. Even with a gap in a painted circle, it represents wholeness to me. I think of myself as a whole person, one who didn't waste the miracle of life. Like many older adults, I have wishes for the future.

Some Wishes

When I drift off to sleep at night or awaken in the morning, I think about my wishes. Maybe some of them will come true.

I wish I could hug my great-grandsons.

I wish I knew how to fold fitted sheets.

I wish I could tell answering machines to press one, two, and three.

I wish I liked cookies less.

I wish cars still had crank windows.

I wish I liked cilantro and fennel.

I wish I were a computer guru.

I wish Alexa would clean my apartment.

My story of renewal continues. I still live in the apartment I shared with John. I still write early in the morning, when the moon is out, as trains blow their whistles, helicopters land on the helipad, and crows swarm into a sky that looks like gray flannel. One thing is different, and it's me. After so much sorrow, my life is filled with surprising, humorous, joyful experiences.

Creating doodle art is a joyful experience from start to finish. Art is more than an expression of feelings; it is an expression of the artist's soul. Every doodle art picture I create is an expression of my soul and the joy I feel inside. My joyous feelings almost leap off the paper. When I look at the pictures I've created, I can hardly believe I made them. But I did, and my quirky, colorful, abstract pictures are proof of healing. "If you've healed yourself, you've done something," I tell myself.

Now you know my story: the sad parts, the glad parts, and the funny parts. After being imprisoned in the darkness of grief, I bask in the brightness of life. Like a potter repairing a broken vase, I gathered the shards—family, friends, education, experience, personality, beliefs, talent—and glued my life back together. The journey was long and the road was bumpy, but I am whole again. I look new and feel new; it's a miracle.

I was worthy of happiness, and you are as well. Stand up to grief and claim happiness for yourself. Though you have doubts, you may be stronger than you realize. There could be a wellspring of strength within you. This brings me back to the decision I made after Helen died:

Death will be the loser. Life will be the winner. I will make it so.

I made it so, and you can too.

Bibliography

American Brain Foundation. "Healing Your Brain After Loss: How Grief Rewires the Brain." September 29, 2021. https://www.americanbrainfoundation.org/how-tragedy-affects-the-brain/.

Beck, Martha. *Finding Your Own North Star: Claiming the Life You Were Meant to Live.* New York: MJF Books. 2001.

Boss, Pauline. *Loving Someone Who Has Dementia: How to Find Hope While Coping with Stress and Grief.* New York: Wiley, 2011.

Deits, Bob. *Life After Loss: A Practical Guide to Renewing Your Life After Experiencing Major Loss.* Boston, MA: Da Capo Lifelong Press. 2009.

Dickinson, Emily. *The Complete Poems.* New York: Little, Brown. 1924.

Frost, Robert. "Bereft." Robertfrost.org. Accessed January 4, 2023. https://www.robertfrost.org/bereft.jsp.

Frost, Robert. "Mending Wall." Robertfrost.org. Accessed January 4, 2023. https://www.robertfrost.org/mending-wall.jsp.

Grollman, Earl A. *Living When a Loved One Has Died.* Boston: Beacon Press. 1995.

Grollman, Earl A. *When Your Loved One is Dying.* Boston: Beacon Press. 1980.

Harper Neeld, Elizabeth. "How Long Is This Grieving Going to Last?" Legacy. January 3, 2017. https://www.legacy.com/news/how-long-is-this-grieving-going-to-last/.

Holinger, Dorothy P. *The Anatomy of Grief: How the Brain, Heart, and Body Can Heal after Loss*. New Haven, CT: Yale University Press. 2020.

Holohan, Meghan. "Study Finds 4 Main Personality Types—Which One Are You?" Today. September 20, 2018. https://www.today.com/health/personality-types-average-self-centered-role-model-or-reserved-t137902.

IESE Business School. "Quality of Life: Everyone Wants It, But What Is It?" *Forbes*, September 4, 2013. https://www.forbes.com/sites/iese/2013/09/04/quality-of-life-everyone-wants-it-but-what-is-it/?sh=3715ce52635d.

Ingram, Katherine. *Grief Girl's Guide*. Lodestone Press. 2020.

Kalidasa. "Look to this Day." 4–5th century AD.

Kenison, Katrina. *The Gift of an Ordinary Day: A Mother's Memoir*. New York: Grand Central Publishing. 2009.

Kessler, David. *Finding Meaning: The Sixth Stage of Grief*. New York: Scribner, 2019.

Kottler, Jeffrey A. *The Language of Tears*. New York: Wiley, 1996.

Kross, Ethan. *Chatter: The Voice in Our Head, Why It Matters, and How to Harness It*. London: Ebury Publishing, 2021.

Marks, Jay W. "Medical Definition of ICU Psychosis." MedicineNet. June 3, 2021. https://www.medicinenet.com/icu_psychosis/definition.htm.

Myers, Edward. *When Parents Die: A Guide for Adults*. New York: Penguin Publishing Group. 1997.

O'Donohue, John. *To Bless the Space Between Us: A Book of Blessings*. New York: Doubleday, 2008.

Ostaseski, Frank. *The Five Invitations: Discovering What Death*

Can Teach Us About Living Fully. New York: Flatiron Books. 2017.

Piderman, Katherine quoted in Dana Sparks. "Mayo Mindfulness: Defining Spirituality." Mayo Clinic News Network. June 19, 2019. https://newsnetwork.mayoclinic.org/discussion/mayo-mindfulness-defining-spirituality-2/.

Rando, Therese A. *How to Go On Living When Someone You Love Dies*. New York: Random House, 1991.

Sharpe, Rachel. "Mindful Living: 16 Ways to Live Mindfully in 2022." Declutter the Mind. September 22, 2020. https://declutterthemind.com/blog/mindful-living/.

Sood, Amit. *The Mayo Clinic Guide to Stress-Free Living*. New York: Hachette Books, 2013.

Sood, Amit. *The Mayo Clinic Handbook for Happiness: A Four-Step Plan for Resilient Living*. New York: Hachette Books. 2015.

Tatelbaum, Judy. *The Courage to Grieve: The Classic Guide to Creative Living, Recovery, and Growth Through Grief*. New York: HarperCollins. 2009.

"Trees Make Wonderful Gifts," The Trees Remember, accessed December 15, 2022, https://thetreesremember.com/.

Villines, Zawn. "What is Ageism, and How Does It Affect Health?" Medical News Today. November 3, 2021. https://www.medicalnewstoday.com/articles/ageism.

Viorst, Judith. *Nearing Ninety: And Other Comedies of Late Life*. New York: Simon & Schuster. 2019.

Acknowledgments

Many dear people made *Winning* possible. I'm grateful to the following people for their kindness and help.

Neil Chethik, editor of Open to Hope for suggesting I write a memoir. I appreciate your wisdom and support.

Dr. Heidi Horsley and Dr. Gloria Horsley for asking me to serve as Assistant Editor of the Open to Hope website. Your job offer came just at the right time.

Editor Andrea Vande Vorde for her patience and meticulous work. You helped me smooth rough spots in the manuscript and review grammar and formatting rules.

Rebecca Lown for her striking cover. I think her cover is eye-catching and represents the book well.

Amy Hodgson for calling me every evening after John died, for her ideas and insights, and for being the best travel companion ever.

My twin grandchildren for their love and understanding. You are outstanding adults and I'm immensely proud of you!

The members of my extended family for their love and care. Special thanks to Dr. Stephen Hodgson and his wife, Eleanor Hodgson, for all the dinners you gave me and the gift of listening.

Terri Leidich, owner and publisher of WriteLife, for believing in *Winning* and publishing my previous books. I'm honored to work with you.

Rave Reviews Book Club for your unfailing support. I'm proud to be a life member of RRBC.

The Lobby Ladies, and one Lobby Lad, for your support, stories, and laughter. You changed my life and made it better.

Charter House for providing a safe and vibrant place for me to live.

Mayo Clinic for saving John's life twice and my life twice. You enabled us to have more loving years together.

More Healing Books by
Harriet Hodgson

Just like you, Harriet Hodgson has lost loved ones. Just like you, she sought help. When Harriet couldn't find the help she wanted, she wrote *Daisy a Day*, 365 short readings about coping with grief. Her tender, thoughtful words can help you find your healing path and keep walking toward the future. *Daisy a Day* is the hug you need.

From the very first page, *Grief Doodling* invites action. Topics range from the benefits of doodling, to why doodling is fun, to doodling tips and responding to doodling prompts. The prompts, based on grief research, promote self-worth and healing. This is a hopeful book, something all grieving kids need.

"Will I survive?" "Will I ever be happy again?" Questions that Harriet Hodgson asked herself after she was left to raise her twin grandchildren while grieving for four family members, including her daughter.

In this book, Harriet reminds us that we are not alone in our grief and, though losses may define our lives, they will not destroy us.

About the Author

Harriet Hodgson has been a freelancer for forty-four years and is the author of thousands of articles and forty-five books. Harriet understands grief all too well. She is a bereaved wife, mother, daughter, sister, daughter-in-law, niece, friend, and pet owner.

Harriet has a BS in Early Childhood Education from Wheelock College of Education and Human Development, an MA in art education from the University of Minnesota, and is a certified art therapy coach. She is a member of the Association of Health Care Journalists, Alliance of Independent Authors, and the Minnesota Coalition for Death Education and Support.

Harriet has appeared on more than 190 talk shows, dozens of BlogTalkRadio shows, and television stations including CNN. A popular speaker, she has given presentations at public health, nursing, Alzheimer's, caregiving, and bereavement conferences. She has also given Zoom workshops about grief doodling and affirmation writing as forward steps on one's healing path.

When Hodgson isn't writing, she is creating doodle art. The award-winning author lives in Rochester, Minnesota. Please visit www.harriethodgson.net for more information about this grandmother, great-grandmother, community volunteer, author, artist, and speaker.